Abraham Lincoln

Abraham Lincoln

by James Daugherty

Illustrated
with lithographs in two colors by the author

BEAUTIFUL FEET BOOKS
SAN LUIS OBISPO, CALIFORNIA

First Published November 1943
Copyright ©1943 By James Daugherty
Originally lithographed in the United States by W.C.D. Glaser
©2008 Beautiful Feet Books
All rights reserved. No part of this publication may be reproduced in any
form without written permission of the publisher.
Library of Congress Control Number 2008937966
ISBN 978-1-893103-32-0

Beautiful Feet Books
1306 Mill Street
San Luis Obispo, CA 93401
www.bfbooks.com
800.889.1978

To Lieutenant Charles M. Daugherty
American soldier-artist
and
his comrades in arms throughout the world

IT was certain that out of the womb of American Democracy
A man should come to the nineteenth century,
The common normal type in full stature, of the casual humorous
    pioneer,
Not in the land-frontier sense merely but much more in horizons
    infinite,
A familiar person, ingenious in all Yankee capacities for all dilemmas,
A young growing tree, a slow sounder-out of meanings and drifts
In a time of confusion or any time in the troubled birth of the Union.

He did not hail from the smug colonial strip, the eastern slopes
He had no credentials from the tide-water plantations
He was not a son of the New England Dynasty.
He came as an axeman from the cabins, a flatboatman out of the great
    central valley,
A slow plowman out of the heart of the continental plain,
Coming as a laugher, a poet, a clown, an artist in the humanities.
Growing up rankly with the border towns, standing on the side lines,
A mediocrity in the rank and file, not a success, not a failure,
A long listener to striving voices, north, south, east, and west.

And now the drawling voice of the all-inclusive tolerant average man

Weighing the reasons in a balance, speaking out as the voice of Truth,

Clear and cool over the troubled land in time of peril,

All lost if the sacred Union is lost,

And the land and the people of the land saying,

This is he for whom we have waited

A man to be lifted up

By the choice and faith of the people

Exalted and alone to bear the intolerable burden and crown of thorns,

Never too exalted to be the compassionate individual friend.

Hated, threatened, reviled more bitterly by his own than by the enemy

Till weary, triumphant and purified at last

Joining an immortal army of farmer boys forever marching into the
    western sky.

Abraham Lincoln—he who happened to be a little more than another

The average all-inclusive type of tolerant democratic man.

JAMES DAUGHERTY

Weston, Connecticut,

May 1943

Contents

Abraham Lincoln

WHEN Daniel Boone, all shaggy and lean, came out of the wilderness, the news went up and down the Valley of Virginia—millions of acres of fat good lands beyond the Cumberland Gap over the blue Alleghenies.

It is said that Daniel Boone, the Long Hunter, told Grandfather Abraham about the land and the game in Kentucky, in the West. The movers, the restless men, the land-hungry families, were crossing the ranges of the Clinch and the Powell, were filing through the Cumberland Gap, stumbling over the Wilderness Road to stake out Kentucky acres in the wilderness.

Among the movers, the walkers, the riders, were Father and Mother Abraham Lincoln with their six children. Little Tom Lincoln was the baby.

Somewhere in the procession rode Lucy Hanks of Virginia, with her baby in her arms. The baby's name was Nancy.

They all climbed through the Cumberland Gap and stumbled over the Wilderness Road into the sunset.

Abraham built a cabin in the clearing. Mother Lincoln spun flax, made soap, and wove, with all the little Lincolns helping, while Father Abraham cleared the trees and the stumps, weary acre by acre, and plowed and planted the rich black loam.

Behind the green forest leaves were the red-skinned watchers, waiting for the moment when the plowman came within musket range and his broad back made an easy mark.

Father Abraham died in his boots with an Indian bullet through his back. It was a memory and a legend and a history in the Lincoln family. Long decades later, after his grandson had died from a bullet in the back, Dennis Hanks told the story. Grandfather Abraham with his three boys had been building a rail fence in a newly cleared field and was lifting the last, the eighth, rail into place when he was dropped by a bullet from the forest ambush. The Indian rushed out and grabbed little Thomas. The two older boys jumped the fence and ran for the stockade. Mordecai reached safety first, and sighting his rifle through a pivot hole in the log fort, drew a bead on the shining silver ornament that hung on the Indian's breast and fired. The Indian dropped Thomas and ran into the forest. Following the trail of blood next day, they found the Indian—dead. It was one of many stories of the dark and bloody ground on the Kentucky frontier.

Little Tom Lincoln and Nancy Hanks grew up on the wild, hard-toiling border. They grew tall and strong on the banks of the Licking River in new Kentucky. Tom married Nancy in the spring, and they rode off to build a cabin and make a clearing and start a family in the land of promise.

They rode down a forest trail to Elizabethtown, or "E town" as it was called for short, where a carpenter like young Tom could work at building cabins, churches, jails, and schools, or make a finely joined table or chair to last a hundred years or more. Here came to Nancy and Tom the new wonder of a baby girl. They called her Sarah. The Lincolns now moved over near Hodgenville. Thomas tried his hand at farming, and built a cabin a couple of miles out of town. In the rough dirt-floored cabin a second baby came to Nancy on February 12, 1809. He squalled, and when he opened his eyes his proud father and mother marveled at his beauty and cleverness. They named him Abraham after his grandfather who had been killed by the Indians.

When little Abe was about two years old, the Lincolns moved again, and built a cabin on Knob Creek, about ten miles from where Abe was born. Near the cabin was Muldraugh's Hill, and the new home was beside the road that ran from Louisville to Nashville. When Abe's mother stood in the cabin door, shading her eyes against the sun with her hand, little Sarah and Abe peeped from behind her skirts and watched freighted wagons and reeling stagecoaches, riders and walkers and tired soldiers from New Orleans drift past. Sarah and Abe and their playmate, Austin Gollaher, were happy paddling in the cool shallows of Knob Creek, hunting out crawfish and mussels, and exploring the endless adventure and mystery of running water. At bedtime they saw the moon over Muldraugh's Hill through the cabin door.

Indiana — 1816

THERE was talk going around Hardin County, Kentucky, that across the Ohio, in southern Indiana, there was good land and plenty of it to be had from the Government (Congress land they called it) for $2 an acre.

The Lincolns' two hundred and thirty acres in Kentucky had not panned out well. When spring floods came down, Knob Creek went on the rampage and carried off young crops along with the good topsoil. Tom Lincoln traded his farm and cabin for four hundred gallons of whisky in barrels. The stuff was a kind of currency along the border, which he could use for trade and barter. He didn't care much for "corn likker" himself.

He made a flatboat of yellow poplar, loaded her with the whisky and his tools, and started down the Rolling Fork toward the Ohio. The boat upset, and the precious tools were lost with some of the whisky. Things like that would happen. He landed on the Indiana shore at Thompson's Ferry, left his salvaged whisky at Mr. Posey's farm near by, and went on a day's journey through the timber. On Pigeon Creek he staked out eighty acres where the forest floor was rich with the leaf mulch of years.

Tom came back to Kentucky to take Nancy and Sarah and little Abe on a hundred-mile journey to their new land in the Indiana wilderness. The Lincolns took from the Knob Creek cabin what things they could carry on the backs of two horses, climbed up, with Sarah and Abe, on their broad backs, looked back at the little home with a tear, and rode off toward the river. They were off again, movers down a forest trail bright with autumn foliage. They reached the river at last, and looked with awe on the vast smooth water winding between the noble hills. As they crossed on the slow ferry Abe looked up and down its long curve, and wondered if he would ever find where it came from and where it went.

From Posey's farm, where Tom had left his belongings on his first trip, by wagon they made the sixteen-mile journey to Pigeon Creek in a day. They found a little hill in the still autumn woods, and built a lean-to, a two-faced cabin, between two trees, with a place for a log fire on the open side, facing south. The towering trees dropped red and yellow leaves of oak and maple, hickory and walnut, on the little shelter where the Lincoln family broke the primeval stillness with the echoing stroke of a broad ax and the sharp crack of a Kentucky rifle.

So the pioneers came across the broad water into the land of promise, with their dreams and plans for abundance and prosperity on their forest acres.

The fat black bear found a winter bed in a hidden cave, the squirrel stored nuts in a hollow tree, the grouse and wild turkey pecked at the seed berries in the underbrush, and the deer moved along southern slopes. In the ancient wisdom of the wilderness, furred and feathered citizens made ready for the cruel armies of the frost and snow.

The wolves of the North Wind moaned and clashed among the branches, and January blizzards buried the land under the deep, soft snow. The pale February sun climbed in the southern sky, tracing blue shadow-patterns of icy branches on the dazzling whiteness of a frozen fairyland.

A red fox, crossing the clearing, made a firebrand on the blue-white snow, and the beating wings of the clamorous crows marked an ebony rhythm against the gray sky.

But sun or snow, day and night, the fire on the open side of the lean-to was fed with oak and hickory and walnut log and limb. Before its limpid flame Nancy roasted the forest game that Tom brought in, and the heavy bearskin and deer pelts kept out the fierce teeth of the cold through the long nights.

The slow spring came, whispering hope and promise through the melting snows. It filled the hungry streams with angry rush of waters that overflowed and covered the lowlands. The skunk cabbage sprang up in the deep swamp and the hinterlands were a sea of mud. Then there were perfect days of soft green, and a wind from the south, when Sarah and Abraham walked barefoot through soft April. In May they went hand in hand down a woodland trail to the "blab" school to learn readin', writin', and cipherin'. In July the corn climbed high toward the blistering sun, and the flies and fierce mosquito hordes tormented man and beast. Autumn brought the blessing of a fruitful year, the full-eared corn, the wild honey and the juicy sweetness of the hickory and walnut. The children found treasure under the butternut tree, and the wild persimmon dropped its strange soft fruit. The leaves of the trees clapped their bright stained hands, and cast off their robes of scarlet and gold onto the rustling forest floor. So the gaunt and golden splendors of the months marched by the cabin door, and over the rolling hills of southern Indiana.

Slowly Thomas raised the walls of his one-roomed log cabin, and laid the long hand-split shingles on the roof. The chimney and fireplace were of sticks and mud. There was a sleeping-loft, with pegs in the wall for Abe to climb up to his bed in the attic. The light came through one window. Instead of glass there was a thin leaf of hog fat which let through a mellow light. More settlers were coming from Kentucky—Nancy's relatives of the clan of Sparrow, Tom and Betsy Sparrow, and seventeen-year-old Dennis Hanks, Nancy's cousin. They lived in the Lincoln lean-to until they built a cabin.

Tom and Betsy took sick. The Lincolns helped, and Nancy watched and tended them as well as her own. The malady worked swiftly, and both of the Sparrows died. Nancy sickened with the same disease. Within a week, she too had gone. Tom Lincoln and Dennis Hanks made a third plank coffin, and buried Nancy in a grave on a hill. The deer left light tracks on the new-made graves.

Weeks later, Parson Elkin, the traveling preacher, came, and prayed and read the Bible over the graves. The wilderness was cruel. The graves of pioneer women were a price and a memory in the eyes of sad men on a lonely wayfaring toward the sunset.

In fathomless wells of pain and grief glinted light of stars, and a voice saying, "And I will pray the Father, and He shall give you another Comforter, that he may abide with you for ever; Even the Spirit of truth; whom the world cannot receive, because it seeth him not, neither knoweth him: but ye know him; for he dwelleth with you, and shall be in you. I will not leave you comfortless: I will come to you."

Fourteen-year-old Sarah Lincoln cooked for Abe and Dennis in the lonely cabin where the sweet presence of Nancy's love seemed to linger and to soften with a bright memory the slow-healing sorrow. But the children went unkempt and ragged without the care of her ministering hands.

Thomas Lincoln had gone back to Kentucky. He could not face the future alone, and had remembered a woman back in Kentucky. When at last he drove into the clearing of the Pigeon Creek farm, he brought with him his new wife, Sarah Bush, who was to be the stepmother of Sarah and Abe. With her were her own three children by her former husband. These were John, Sarah, and Matilda Johnston. Thomas had courted Sarah Bush long ago in their youth, but they had parted, and had each married. When Thomas needed a helper to carry on the home in the wilderness, he remembered Sarah Bush. He had heard that she was a widow in Elizabethtown, Kentucky. The widow Sarah Bush Johnston had agreed to his proposal, and after certain business arrangements, they were married. She was a woman with an understanding heart, wide and deep enough to bind up the deep wounds of childhood grief. They unloaded chairs and a bureau from the wagon, tools of use and comfort in a frontier home. There were five growing children in the cabin now, but Mother Sarah helped to keep them all happy and busy.

Abe was old enough to help his father and learn to handle tools, the way and knack of ax, hoe, plow—each had a special cunning. Sheep, pigs, horse, and cows were fellow creatures who had their own needs and cares for comfort and protection. There were long days of hard physical labor from sunup to sundown for all of them. It was easy to sleep when they turned in at night.

As he worked alone in the tall timber, Abe made acquaintance with the forest singers and talkers. He listened to the woodpecker's drum, and the redbird's rich note, the wood dove's melancholy cry, the cheery quails' "bob white," the harsh clamor of the crows, the blue jay's scolding whine, and the meadow lark's free ecstasy. He could read in the soft earth or snow shorthand autobiographies written by the deer, the wolf, and the ambling bear. He could say to the veined hands of the leaf multitude, I know you and all your family. He knew the good snakes from the bad, and dealt swiftly with the rattler and the deadly copperhead.

His bare feet and hands grew strong and hard. They were quick, sure workers and travelers, which hung loose and supple on long, tough arms and legs, taking their orders from a high, hard noodle, perched on a leather-brown neck. From under a crow's nest of coarse black mane, drooping gray eyes looked out of deep sockets at the dream of things, at the friendly world where he was always willing and eager to lend a hand or help a friend. Or if a quarreler was looking for trouble, or anyone wanted a rough and tumble, he could let loose a hurricane of muscle and lean power that was tough as Indianny oak and hickory. About all he really hated was lying and whisky. He had a lonely boy's hunger for people, and was curious about them, too, but in a special sort of way feeling for what they might be thinking. He had a long memory for comic stories. He stored them up until something reminded him. He would tell stories that could make a horse laugh. He was a listener, too, at barbecue, house-raising, and camp meeting, where earnest men and women

prayed and read from the Bible about the wrath and the mystic tenderness of God. He chased new hard words till he caught up with their meanings, and could round them·up in groups and clear sentences.

He was growing up to be one of a hard, lean, frost-bitten, sun-scorched race of men and women who lived under a high bleak sky, with a clean wind blowing from the four corners of a bright new land. A kind of people who had wrastled with long years of fat and lean, blight and bloom, taking the bitter with the sweet, the pain and travail with the laughter and the joy, finding a wine of contentment and a bread that was good. If there were any whiners and complainers, flabby, soft-jowled, paunchy, pasty-faced, indoor bottom-warmers, they didn't last long, not in southern Indianny in the early eighteen hundreds.

Besides the Bible and lawbooks, there were wanderers. A vagabond copy of *Pilgrim's Progress*, a dog-eared *Aesop*, or a worn Weems's *Life of Washington*, strayed over the Alleghenies into Indiana to open up worlds of wonder for a curious, hungry plowboy, eager to learn. That's the way it was with Abe, shaping, changing, and growing through the slow swift years of youth.

The Ferry — 1828

ABE WAS seven years old when he first came to Indiana to the Pigeon Creek farm, and now he was going on eighteen. He had done a powerful lot of stump-pulling, wood-chopping, and cornhusking for folks around Gentryville during that time. Now on his own he had gone down Anderson Creek and built him a snug flatboat to ferry passengers aboard or ashore from the river packets, for whatever he could get. The river was a highway for traffic going up river and down, and a barrier for crossers going North and South. Abe saw fur traders and slave-catchers, movers, gamblers, lawyers, moguls, farmers, all the motley pageant of the rough new country, coming and going in a vast shifting march from old worlds to new. On the river vast flatboats, broadhorns, and arks drifted by on their way downstream to New Orleans, loaded with pork and grain and whisky and ginseng. Round the bend churned high proud steamers, belching sparks and flame from tall black stacks, and trailing long streamers of smoke from their wood-burning engines.

Abe heard tell of Robert Owen bringing his new Social Order to New Harmony, Indiana. His people were to work together and share alike, and there would be books and learning for all. Along the river people laughed about "the boatload of knowledge," as they called it, that was bringing the idealists and their books to the new community.

People shook their heads and talked about Edward Coles, the rich Virginia planter, who had brought his slaves down the Ohio River to southern Illinois, given them their freedom and one hundred and sixty acres of land each, as they wept on their knees with gratitude.

Abe learned about men who put Truth and Liberty above money and profits, and who were scorned and hated for it; men who held lights and torches of Freedom and Faith to shine across dark waters of history and drifting mists of time.

Long after, Lincoln told this story about when he was a boy at Anderson's Creek:

"Well, I was about eighteen years of age. I belonged, you know, to what we call down South the scrubs; people who do not own slaves are nobody there. But we had succeeded in raising, chiefly by my labor, sufficient produce, as I thought, to justify me in taking it down the river to sell. After much persuasion I got the consent of my mother to go and construct a little flatboat, large enough to take a barrel or two of things we had gathered, with myself and little bundle, down to New Orleans.

"A steamer was coming down the river. I was contemplating my new flatboat, and wondering whether I could make it stronger or improve it in any particular, when two men came down to the shore in carriages with trunks, and looking at the different boats, singled out mine, and asked, 'Who owns this?'

"I answered, somewhat modestly, 'I do.'

" 'Will you take us and our trunks out to the steamer?'

" 'Certainly,' said I. I was very glad to have the chance of earning something. I supposed that each of them would give me two or three bits. The trunks were put on my flatboat, the passengers on the trunks, and I sculled them out to the steamboat.

"They got on board, and I lifted up their heavy trunks and put them on the deck. The steamer was about to put on steam again when I called out that they had forgotten to pay me. Each of them took from his pocket a silver half-dollar and threw it on the floor of my boat. I could scarcely believe my eyes as I picked up the money.

"Gentlemen, you may think it was a very little thing, and in these days it seems to me a trifle, but it was a most important incident in my life. I could scarcely credit that I, a poor boy, had earned a dollar in less than a day—that by honest work I had earned a dollar. The world seemed wider and fairer before me. I was a more hopeful and confident being from that time."

About four miles from Abe's home on Little Pigeon Creek lived a prosperous farmer named Gentry, and the crossroads store and village near him were called Gentryville. When Mr. Gentry wanted to sell his crops and herds in the markets of New Orleans, he needed a strong and honest boatman to help his son Allen take a flatboat down the yellow winding way of the treacherous snag-filled Mississippi. He hired young Abe Lincoln because he knew he could trust him, and because Abe had experience at handling river boats.

It was the first time either of the boys had been far from home. As they drifted down the midstream of the broad Ohio, the thousand miles of river faring ahead of them promised high adventure. They drifted on until they came to the great Mississippi, the Father of

Waters. All day long they manned the long sweeps, watching the river ahead for snags and shoals. Old Man River had a thousand tricks and grim traps to shipwreck Indiana greenhorns. At night they set their lines for the big juicy Mississippi catfish that were sometimes as big as a man. They lay on their backs by the fire and watched the red moon rise through the river mist, and the hanging stars burn in the spangled sky. Through hot, slow days they kept the flatboat in mid-channel with the heavy sweeps, eased her round the bends and kept her off sand bars as they sang the river songs, "The Hunters of Kentucky," and others.

At lonely settlements perched on timbered bluffs they heard about Andrew Jackson being elected President. They saw sleepy trading posts on the sugar coast, Memphis, Natchez, Vicksburg. Coming down the river on the high waters of the spring floods were keelboats, broadhorns, arks, sleds, barges, vast lumber rafts, and pirogues or dugout canoes, and little sailing skiffs. They hailed them and swapped river news with raftsmen, settlers, horse-and-alligator men, traders, the gamblers and gypsies of the drifting waterways. They shuddered at ghastly tales of the pirates of Cave in Rock, and heard how the savage Leader Mason had robbed and murdered until the city of Natchez had offered $500 reward for his capture dead or alive. Two of his band brought in his severed head and claimed the prize. Natchez paid the $500 to the pirates, arrested, tried, and hanged them, and returned the $500 to the town. One night the boys awoke to find seven Negroes robbing their boat. In the fight Abe got a scar that he carried for life.

New Orleans was the first big city Abe had ever been in. When they had made the deal for the cargo and boat, they took a look around the gaudy town. Beautiful Creole girls smiled invitingly, and gamblers and card sharks plied their trade in noisy saloons. It was an easy, graceful, languorous, cruel town to open the eyes of a backwoods puritan. They looked it over, and held onto their cash.

They stood in the crowd at the slave market, and watched hard-faced traders bid for black men, women, girls, and boys. Abe had heard plenty about the right and wrong of slavery, but he had never seen men and women sold like cattle on an auction block.

They booked passage upstream on a river steamboat bringing cotton up to St. Louis. Her great paddle wheels bucked the mighty current. Her massive walking beam rose and fell as Negro slaves stoked the fires with pine logs, and the rolling plumes of black smoke from her tall stacks trailed far down the river.

From St. Louis, the boys walked back to Gentryville, with a string of tall tales to tell around the fire in Gentry's store—of what they had seen at first hand in a thousand-mile trip across America and back.

Forever Moving on — 1830

WHEN the boys got back to Gentryville, Abe found the Lincolns and the Hankses and the Halls talking about moving over into Illinois. Abe had lived for fourteen years on the Indiana farm at Little Pigeon Creek. The clan had grown. Abe's stepsisters were married, one to Dennis Hanks; Abe's own sister Sarah had married and died in childbirth. Now they were getting letters from Dennis's brother, John Hanks, about fine farm lands around Decatur, Illinois. John had moved into Illinois from Kentucky, and had built one of the first cabins in Macon County.

The Lincoln tribe decided to pull up stakes and move on toward the ever calling West. That winter Abe helped build an ox wagon, shaping tough timber into a stout, graceful prairie schooner. The family sold their lands and goods, and bought seven yoke of oxen. They loaded their ark with bedding, clothes, tools, kitchen utensils, and the paraphernalia of wayfaring from the beginnings of time.

Sad memories tugged at their hearts as they looked at scenes and landmarks of love, birth, and death for the last time. Slowly the

fourteen oxen strained at their yokes, the bull whips cracked, the axles creaked and asked for more grease, neighbors waved from cabin doors, and the caravan lumbered off.

They were leaving the eastern forest lands and approaching the vast continental plain, where the long stretches of prairie were covered with the wild grass that grew six feet high. At the end of the day's trek they pitched camp near running water, warmed up around the evening cook fire, and after a supper of game and corn pone, slept in the wagon under heavy bearskins.

Abe had just turned twenty-one when they crossed the Wabash, and his rawhide boots for the first time sank deep in the juicy Illinois mud as he trudged along by the spattered ox team. He had bought a peddler's stock for the journey, and stopped at the sparse settlements and cabins along the way to persuade suspicious housewives to buy pins and needles. When at last the travel-worn cavalcade lurched into Decatur, the citizens grinned at the strangers and said they had just four miles to go to John Hanks's place.

After the clan reunion round John's hospitable table, and a rest in real beds again, John Hanks took them six miles farther on to where he had already cut the logs for their new home. Everybody pitched in, and in one day they raised the new cabin.

That spring the men cleared fifteen acres for planting, and Dennis and Abe split rails for a snake fence to go round the new farm. Abe worked hard, clearing land, splitting rails, and breaking the tough sod with a bull-tongued plow.

When winter set in there was deep snow and terrible cold. The driving blizzards covered the land under a deep sheath of white iron. Food and fuel were scarce in the leaky cabins, where the bitter frost crept in and gnawed at the bones of men and women shivering around a feeble blaze. By spring Tom Lincoln had decided he didn't want to face another winter around Decatur, and moved south and east, to Goose Nest Prairie.

ABE WAS twenty-one and his own man. He was no longer Tom Lincoln's boy, to be knocked off a rail fence for having too saucy a tongue. He was free to follow like his fathers before him the endless drift from cabin to cabin toward the West, or he could listen to dreams and voices out of dog-eared books he had read by pine-knot lights, hearing trumpets calling and the voices of many waters. The Father of Waters was calling him now, and he signed up with John Hanks and John Johnston to make another flatboat trip down the Mississippi to carry a cargo for Mr. Denton Offut to New Orleans.

Denton Offut was a talker, a hustler, a boisterous man of large enterprise and confidence which expanded under the influence of whisky. He was looking for a crew to take a flatboat with cargo down the river to New Orleans. John and Abe both knew something of the river. Mr. Offut contracted with them and John Johnston, Abe's stepbrother-in-law, to join him in his enterprise. For a month they worked at building the huge flatboat, getting out their timber from the forest and having it turned into clean fragrant planks at the Prairie Creek sawmill. Abe was full of fun and the high ecstasy of youth and freedom. He kept them all laughing with stories and jokes when the axes and hammers were not swinging. The Sangamon was on its spring rampage when they got the heavy barge into the water. The cargo was hauled up from Beardstown in ox wagons and they loaded the boat deep with barrels of pork, corn, and a fragrant drove of live hogs. They drifted down the rushing river amid the hurrahs and whoops of the old Sangamon settlers on the banks.

They poled down the Sangamon to New Salem and tried to take the deep-laden flatboat over the dam of the Rutledge mill. Half-way over she stuck with the front end hanging over and the back end caught on the dam. All New Salem came out to offer advice and bets and watch the proceedings from the bluff above the dam.

Under Abe's direction the crew shifted the squealing cargo to another boat, bored a hole in the overhanging end, rolled the heavy barrels forward till the water ran out through the hole and she went over into deep water amid cheers from the bluff.

They reloaded and floated on down toward St. Louis, drifted on down the great river in the warm spring sunshine. They passed drowsing river towns and put up at Memphis, Vicksburg, and Natchez. By the time they had reached New Orleans, Mr. Offut was convinced that he had employed a very unusual young man, who was strong and honest as well as entertaining and intelligent.

As John Hanks remembered, "There it was we saw Negroes chained, maltreated, whipped and scourged. Lincoln saw it, his heart bled, said nothing much, was silent from feeling, was sad, looked bad, felt bad, was thoughtful and abstracted. It was on this trip he formed his opinions of slavery. It ran its iron into him then and there."

After winding up their business at New Orleans and taking in the sights of that glamorous city, the three booked passage on an upstream steamboat. At St. Louis they parted. Abe, John Hanks, and Johnston walked back to Illinois, and Offut stayed in St. Louis until he could purchase the goods with which he would start a store in New Salem, whose citizens had showed such interest in his enterprise at the Rutledge dam. Abe would run the store, business would hum, New Salem would boom, Mr. Offut would start a steamboat line up the Sangamon, everyone would get rich and the sun would never set on the prosperity in New Salem.

There are places where the road divides, and good companions say "This is my way" or "I turn off here. God be with you till we meet again." When Abe got back to Illinois, a full-grown man, he went to the Lincoln cabin on Goose Nest Prairie to say good-by to Sally Bush, the pioneer woman who had given him love and understanding ever since he had been a ten-year-old motherless boy. It was not so hard to say good-by to his Pappy. But they gripped hard hands as man to man, forgot old disagreements, and wished each other good luck. At the turn of the road Abe looked back and waved a last farewell to the wistful figures by the cabin door.

Sangamon Spring — 1831

FROM its source near Lake Michigan the Illinois River makes a big bend south across Illinois to the Mississippi. When it meets the Father of Waters it says "Here is a load of the best topsoil in America to help fill up the hole in the bottom of the Gulf of Mexico." Out of the heart of Illinois the Sangamon goes down to join up with the Illinois as a helper. It hurries over the shallows saying "I'll be late," or broods in deep slow channels, whispering "It's good to stay in Illinois, to be a mirror for the harlequin sycamore and the yellow willows under a cobalt sky," or it goes singing by New Salem saying "Howdy do." As the lazy waters of the Sangamon eddied and laughed by New Salem in the July heat they might have said "This day's a day to remember. Today I'm bringing you a boatload of everlasting glory. This morning I'm bringing you Abraham Lincoln paddling his own canoe."

Abe tied up his dugout canoe at the Rutledge dam, put his bundle under his arm, scrambled up the bluffs, and walked into New Salem.

It was election day and there was lots of dust and argument around the post office. The tougher element from Clary's Grove were in town likkering up, and everybody was feeling relaxed and neighborly. It was all new to a backwoods farm hand like Abe, especially the politics. Politics was the big crop in Illinois. It was meat and drink and sport and business. People who wanted to get on, who wanted success and power and grandeur, or just excitement, or just wasting time were mixed up in politics. It was all new to Abe. He began to learn about politics that very first day in New Salem, and he never stopped learning. Abe listened around in the general store and told a funny story about the lizard that got in the preacher's pants. Everybody in the store hollered and laughed and those that hadn't heard it asked him to tell it again. Before sundown people pointed to him and said "That's the feller that told the story about the lizard that got in the preacher's pants." You couldn't say exactly that Abe made friends easily; he really didn't have to *make* friends at all. He was at home with people just the same as he was at home with trees. People all liked this rawboned, long-legged gawker and drawler just as naturally as they liked tall corn or a strong gentle horse.

In the shade of Mr. Offut's new store, long-eared hound-dogs dreamed and scratched fleas. A huge pink sow grunted and sighed in the August heat in a wallow near the door. Venturesome hens pecked at kernels on the doorsill. Inside, Abe weighed sugar, or coffee, and made change. When there were no customers, he would tell a story to the loafers who dropped in to rest their feet on a barrel, squirt tobacco juice at the sawdust-filled spittoon, and talk politics and town gossip with the newcome storekeeper.

Several sway-backed ponies from Clary's Grove, with Roman noses and mustang mustaches, stood by the hitching-post switching flies with their scrawny tails. Mr. Offut was taking bets from a group of loafers that Lincoln, his store clerk, could outsmart, outrun, outfight, and outwrastle anybody in New Salem. Mr. Offut had made claim too often, and the Clary's Grove boys were due in town to see their champion, Jack Armstrong, make mincemeat of Mr. Offut's lanky storekeeper.

The tough element lived about four miles from town at Clary's Grove. They were a rough wild gang of roistering bully boys. The toughest of all was Jack Armstrong. He was the cock of the walk, the fire-eater, strong man, and leader of the gang. Fighting was no stand-up-and-knock-down affair among the horse-and-alligator men of

Sangamon County. It was free and fanciful, and included eye-gouging, ear-chewing, neck-twisting, hair-pulling, butting, kicking, and any new combinations and improvisings that special talents brought forth under pressure.

The Clary's Grove boys rode whooping into town in a wild tornado, likkered up at Clary's grocery, which was next to the Offut store, placed their bets, and called for the new storekeeper to come out and take it.

Abe preferred to sidestep trouble when he could, but this time he would have to take on the wild bull of Sangamon County or else leave town. After a few passes, the two champions lit into each other and the fur began to fly. Jack was short and heavy and he sailed right into Abe's middle. Then something like a bear trap clamped down on him. Something like a hammer and claws, like several tons of rock and a prairie cyclone in one, struck him all of a heap. When Jack began to try a few foul tricks, Abe really got mad, caught him by the neck, and slammed him down. At this point Armstrong's gang decided to take a hand and closed in to save Jack's remains. Abe backed up against the cabin wall and held off the mob with his long arms, but it was looking bad for the new storekeeper. Armstrong jumped up, broke through the fray, reached out an open hand to Lincoln, and said, "You're the best feller that ever broke into this settlement."

The fight was over. As the dust settled there was rough horseplay and laughter. Abe belonged. He was one of the gang. They knew that he was a mighty powerful wrastler and storyteller, and these things went a long way in New Salem.

If Abe won over the roughs and toughs of Clary's Grove in the Jack Armstrong match, there were other men in the little settlement whom he sought out for their strength of character and spiritual light. There was the frontier schoolmaster, Mentor Graham, who taught students for five cents a day, the quiet scholar to whom

Lincoln went for help over the hard places in arithmetic and survey-ing, or the *Kirkham's Grammar* that he had walked six miles to borrow. There was the faithful country doctor, John Allen, who day and night ministered to the sick, and turned all the fees for Sunday calls over to the church. He had started the first Sunday-school in New Salem, and the first temperance society. Another spir-itual warrior was Old John Berry, "the noblest Roman of them all," a brave and stanch apostle who people said was the man who had done most to Christianize southern Illinois. Abe liked to visit with Justice Bowling Green, the paunchy justice of the peace, who weighed two hundred and fifty pounds and roared and shook at Lincoln's stories. He could answer Abe's questions about what was right and wrong in the eyes of the law and the statutes of the State of Illinois.

Different from all these was shiftless Jack Kelso, the inveterate fisherman and hunter and lover of John Barleycorn. Under the sycamores by the bass pools, Abe listened to him recite the songs of Bobby Burns and long rhythms of blank verse from Shakespeare's plays. For the first time Abe heard thought woven into a music of words that had warm human appeal and magic power that reached the heart. These men opened windows of light and doors of the mind to a backwoods farm hand searching after wisdom and hun-gering after knowledge. Thus Abe's groping mind was fed and clothed and comforted at the cabin hearthstones of a village school-master, a country doctor, a circuit preacher, a Falstaffian justice of the peace, and a learned ne'er-do-well.

During the day, Abe was supposed to be selling merchandise at Denton Offut's store. Under the counter was a handy corner where Abe kept the *Kirkham's Grammar*. When there were no customers, which was pretty often, he had Slicky Bill Greene hear him recite exercises in the ways and habits of verbs, adverbs, and modifying clauses. Bill Greene was the young man Offut had hired as Abe's assistant. They both slept in the loft over the store. Bill snored nobly while Abe studied *Kirkham's Grammar* or some other borrowed treasure far into the night.

When Abe heard that Mr. Rutledge, who owned the mill and the tavern, was starting a debating society, he dropped around one evening and took a hand in the argument. Afterward some of the debaters said, "You wouldn't have thought the feller down at Offut's store could talk such horse sense."

Down at Offut's store time stood still, or loafed, sitting on a sugar barrel. Trade was petering out in spite of Abe's stories, or because of them—it didn't matter which. Abe would knock off for horse races, wrestling matches, gander-pullings, or to umpire at bully fights, and watch on the side lines at cockfights when the bets ran high. He always remembered the time when Babb McNabb threw his prize white rooster into the ring for the fight and the rooster turned tail and scooted out of the ring, mounted a fence at a safe distance, flapped his wings, and crowed valiantly. As McNabb ruefully paid his lost bets, he said, "Yes, you little cuss, you're great on dress parade, but you're not worth a damn when it comes to a fight."

There were more respectable jollifications and occasions where people were well behaved. Abe lent a hand at the barbecues and house-raisin's, and looked on at camp meetings where Peter Cartwright, the pioneer Methodist minister, exhorted the faithful until they got "the jerks." Some of the congregation brought corn likker in little brown jugs. People had strong opinions about whether whisky was a good or a bad thing. When the Baptist church dismissed two members, one for joining Dr. Allen's temperance society and another for drunkenness, a man stood up in meeting, held up a whisky bottle, and said, "Brethering, seems like you ain't at all 'sistent when you throws out one brother for getting tight and another for taking the pledge. Now, Brethering, just how much of this here critter have I got to drink to be in good standing in this here church?"

Election time was the most exciting of all. It was personal popularity rather than party that was the best asset for a candidate around New Salem. It didn't matter a lot who was Whig and who was Democrat. People usually voted for the man they liked best on his personal merits.

When it came time for candidates to step out, people said "Abe, why don't you try? Everybody likes you." When Abe asked Mentor Graham and his wise friends about it, they said it was a great idea and they all got their heads together and helped Abe get up a speech —about how he was in favor of straightening out the Sangamon River for steamboat navigation, which everybody was for, and for reducing the interest rates on debts, which a lot of people who owed money thought was a fine idea, and of course he said he was for more free education.

Just as folks were getting warmed up about the campaign, news came in that made people forget even politics. It was war, and a call for volunteers, Indians on the warpath, burning and murdering along the Rock River in northwestern Illinois.

New Salem Volunteers

BLACK HAWK, the chief of the Sac Indians, had come back across the Mississippi with five hundred braves in war paint to take back the burial grounds of their people. Though they had bargained with the whites and made treaties, Black Hawk now claimed that his lands could not be sold. Only things that can be carried away can be sold. He spoke out of the ancient wisdom of the primitive peoples:

"My reason teaches me that land cannot be sold. The Great Spirit gave it to his children to live upon, and cultivate, as far as is necessary, for their subsistence, and so long as they occupy and cultivate it they have the right to the soil, but if they voluntarily leave it then another people have a right to settle upon it. Nothing can be sold but such things as can be carried away."

But white settlers thought differently; promoters and land speculators thought that Indians interfered with the free play of private enterprise, depreciated land values, and prevented the improvement of property. If Black Hawk didn't understand about real-estate deals, it was just too bad for the Indians. The United States Government was sending troops and calling for a volunteer State Militia.

Of course everybody who could tote a gun in New Salem joined up to form a company. Each man brought along his own gun, ammunition, and equipment. The company democratically elected its own captain. Lincoln and the Clary's Grove boys volunteered. Instead of being elected to the legislature, Abe found himself elected captain of the volunteers, "a success that gave me more pleasure than any I have had since," he once wrote to a friend.

Somehow the New Salem Volunteers never caught up with Black Hawk, or fought Indians. They marched across northern Illinois, had weeks of rough campaigning crowded with grotesque adventures and comedies of error. Captain Lincoln came back to New Salem from the wars with a knapsack full of tall tales about the bloodless campaign, in which he poked fun at himself. He had made new friends, had grown, and learned about farm-boy soldiers in a tough democratic army, marching on through the gray rain, sleeping on the ground, taking hardships uncomplaining, laughing with a fierce undisciplined bravado. They were made of the same stuff that had marched at Concord and Bunker Hill, crossed the Delaware on an icy winter night, and shivered at Valley Forge.

Abe had filed away another book of sharp memory pictures whose clear details never grew dim with long passing years.

My Politics Are Short and Sweet — 1832

LINCOLN got back to town just two weeks before the election, so he had to pitch in and get votes. He went from door to door, helped gangs of men in the field with hay or wheat, or took on a wrestling champion. It ended up after an auction at Pappsville. There was a big crowd calling for him to make a speech. Just as he started to speak, a fight broke out in the crowd. He got off the stump, grabbed the orneriest scrapper by the seat of his pants and the scruff of his neck, and threw him out. Then he went on with the speech.

"I have been solicited by many friends to become a candidate for the legislature. My politics are short and sweet, like the old woman's dance. I am in favor of a national bank. I am in favor of the internal-improvements system and a high protective tariff. These are my sentiments and political principles. If elected I shall be thankful; if not, it will be all the same."

Everybody came to town on the big day to vote. Of course everybody in New Salem and the Clary's Grove boys had voted for him. In his precinct the vote was 277 for him and 7 against. But he was not well enough known outside of his own district to carry the county, and he was only twenty-three. "But it was the only time Abraham was ever beaten by the direct vote of the people."

Abe had not only lost in the elections; Offut's store had finally petered out, and he was out of a job. He thought about taking up blacksmithing—he had the arms for it. He had always dreamed of being a lawyer, but there was so much yet that he had to learn. One day Abe heard that the Clary's Grove boys had smashed up a store to settle a grudge against the owner. He and young Berry had sauntered down to see the store and found Bill Greene had bought out the owner, who had left town in disgust. Lincoln and Berry decided to go into business. They borrowed the money, bought out Bill Greene, and put up the sign of the firm of Berry & Lincoln.

There was no rush of business, only a fine crop of debts getting bigger. Abe was around talking politics or with his nose in a book. Poor Berry, the minister's son, was a victim of the drink habit. In a short time Abe sold out his share to his partner. Corn likker was doing a lot of damage around New Salem. Women didn't like the idea of Sam Hill, the postman, running a saloon. He was ousted, and Lincoln was appointed postmaster.

It wasn't much of a job. Mail to New Salem was not very heavy, so Abe had plenty of time to read and to pick up a dollar at odd jobs in the neighborhood. As he went around, he would carry the mail in his hat to make a rural delivery. He got the habit of keeping things under his hat.

Friends who were glad to help him got him an appointment as deputy surveyor for the county. He had to sit up late nights, with Mentor Graham helping him learn about the art of surveying out of the books. He liked things that were straight and exact. He soon made a good surveyor. He was pleased to find that surveyors and postmasters get to meet and talk to a lot of voters in a friendly sort of way. His debts in connection with the Berry & Lincoln store had not been straightened out, and when Berry died, Abe found that he owed $1100. People often got out of such scrapes by leaving town. Abe paid up as best and when he could. It took him fifteen years.

When the 1834 elections came around, the Democrats asked Abe to be their candidate, although he was a Whig. Everybody was for him, Whig or Democrat. He made stump speeches, told stories, and helped pitch hay. Winning this time was a foregone conclusion, and he came out at the head of the list. Best of all, he had interested a shrewd Springfield lawyer, John T. Stuart, who urged him to study law and lent the books and hinted that when he was admitted to the bar he would help him get started in Springfield. That summer Abe spent his time around New Salem lost in a lawbook, sitting in the shade with his feet in the air and his nose in Blackstone. Offut and

Stuart were men who had led opportunity up to his door, and when it knocked he had been ready to say "Here I come."

It was getting time for Abe to go down to Vandalia to the General Assembly. But he couldn't wear that old straw hat that carried the mail and those funny linen pants held up by one unreliable suspender. Besides, the pants were six inches too short and showed his bare shins above the tops of his blue yarn socks sticking up out of his huge yellow brogans. So his friends fixed him up in a new store suit and lent him his fare and sent him off with a big cheer on the rattling stage going south toward Vandalia.

The Vandalia Stage — 1834

ABE drew his long legs up till his bony knees nearly touched his chin as he sat on the cramped seat in the stage, jolting over the rutty road.

Could it be only three years since he had said good-by to Mother Sarah Bush and had drifted down to New Salem out of the wilderness, an unschooled farmhand out of a backwoods clearing, a hired laborer just off a flatboat? Could it really be twenty-five-year-old Abe Lincoln going down to the General Assembly of the State of Illinois as the elected representative of the people? What in all his abysmal ignorance did he know about laws, economics, finance, and state politics? But he could learn and listen, as he had learned from Mentor Graham, Dr. Allen, Bowling Green, and Jack Kelso, as he had learned from the people of Sangamon.

The raw December wind blew across the level fields of stubble, rustling in the dry blades of the fodder shocks and whispering among the tepees of the Indian corn, whispering "First the blade, then the ear, after that the full grain in the ear." The Vandalia stage rattled over the long prairie miles carrying a lean learner, a slow grower, a gloomy laugher, on toward a high, sad, violent fate.

43

The newcomer from Sangamon, loitering and listening in the hotels and at the State House, was learning, was learning the ropes, the complicated wheels of politics and party deals, of logrolling and back-scratching in the trade and compromise of party maneuver and strategy. He watched the passion and greed of self-interest pushing or jockeying for position and pelf.

In noisy boardinghouses he sat at crowded tables and told stories, or dropped in at the famous Cass Emporium to hear Mr. Cass bet that there wasn't an article you could name that he didn't have in his store. He joined in the laugh when a man took the bet and asked for a goose yoke. Mr. Cass produced a fantastic contraption which he said was a goose yoke that he kept for legislators. Abe was always an easy mixer, and fitted quietly into the boisterous gaiety of the young capital.

There were social events attended by high-steppers from the first families of Kentucky bringing an easy grace and proud airs to crude Vandalia. Abe was a wondering gawker at brilliant parties where there was music, and bright lights and the color and glamour of scented beauty and high gallantry in silk and lace.

The town was full of the strange contrasts of a new country, filling up with drifters, movers, boosters, with aristocrats and blue-bloods from Kentucky. Sometimes he would spend long evenings of serious talk with a circuit preacher, or again listen to a friend make mountain music on a Carolina fiddle.

He was asked to political banquets where the tables groaned with prairie fatness and rare wine flowed like the Sangamon. As the night grew late and fun waxed furious, he saw Stephen Douglas and James Shields mount the table and dance down its long length in each other's arms amid the roar of cheers and the crash of glass and china. He was working and playing in the boisterous hurly-burly of a frontier democracy growing up with a fierce energy into an empire of wealth and power.

It was a new country. As for his being born in a log cabin, every white person born west of the Alleghenies had been born in a log cabin or a log fort. It was a young man's world. The Constitution of the United States itself was not fifty years old.

He took a hand in the action and debate of the turbulent legislature as he came back for three successive terms as the representative from Sangamon. He was learning the curious ways by which the elected representatives of the people carried on the government in a democracy.

As a result of the internal-improvement system, the iron horse was rolling into Illinois snorting with prosperity and boom times. The sky was the limit for enterprise and gilded speculations. The legislature at Vandalia waved their hats, got aboard the band wagon, and voted charters, bridges, highways, and tollgates to bring good times and big money to the lean young State of Illinois. Abe too thought it was fine and went along with the big parade. He had always been for "internal improvements." When the Assembly passed a resolution saying "We highly disapprove of Abolition societies," Abe went on record that he could stand out against the crowd for his convictions. He stated that he did not approve of Abolition societies, but he believed that slavery was wrong, and he protested because the resolution didn't say so.

Although Illinois had come into the Union as a Free State, most people in the southern part of the state were movers from Kentucky, and many were pro-slavery in sentiment. They made things rough for the Abolitionists. A brave man named Elijah Lovejoy, who had been driven out of St. Louis for publishing an antislavery paper, was killed by a mob in Alton, Illinois, for persisting in his attempt to publish an Abolitionist paper.

The Assembly was going to change the capital from Vandalia to somewhere nearer the center of the state. There were a number of struggling towns which needed the prosperity and wealth that the capital would bring. There was a hot fight on in the legislature as to which town would get the prize. There was logrolling, lobbying, trading, and maneuvering among rival groups. Lincoln had become adept at political strategy, just as he had mastered *Kirkham's Grammar* or the rules of surveying. He was the leader of a group of nine six-footers from Sangamon who found that by sticking and voting together, one for all and all for one, they could swing things when the vote was close. They were called the Long Nine. It was said that in the final vote it was due to the Long Nine that Springfield was chosen to be the permanent capital. In the summer of 1837 at the barbecues, fairs, and celebrations around Springfield, there were cheers and toasts and speeches in honor of the Long Nine.

Things were looking mighty bright for a self-taught young man who had just been admitted to the bar and asked into the office of John Stuart as junior partner in the new firm of Stuart & Lincoln, in Springfield, Illinois. He went back to New Salem to say good-by to the loyal friends who were so proud and happy in his success. They figured he was a good sample of what New Salem could turn out.

All he owned would be in the saddlebags he was putting on the borrowed nag he was going to ride to Springfield. All except his debts. But it was April and the world was full of new beginnings. There would be friends and opportunity waiting for him, and already he was known to the political bigwigs. He was going to be a lawyer, and the law was the highway to success. Nearly all the positions of power in politics and government were held by lawyers.

So he laughed, and waved a last good-by as he dug his heels in the bony ribs of the borrowed nag and galloped lickety-split down the hill toward Springfield.

LONG after the lights had gone out forever in the deserted cabins on the New Salem bluff, and when a tragic glory hung about his name and fame, recorders came to the old scenes seeking out the men and women Lincoln had known and loved in the vanished cabins and the haunted paths where he had walked, asking Why was he sad? What was he like? What made him weep? What made him laugh? What was his secret? Whom did he love? What did he hate?

Men and women, searching in the twilight attic of past years, dusted off daguerreotypes of memory, and repeated the echoes of his remembered phrases, recalling the old jests and laughter, and restoring the colors of pictures faded and darkened by time.

One memory story tells of Ann, the golden-haired daughter of old James Rutledge, who had owned the mill and tavern at New Salem.

Lincoln and Ann had known each other. The gentle girl had touched and sounded depths of yearning tenderness in his gaunt and lonely soul. They had been drawn toward each other and had fallen in love. There was a man to whom Ann had been engaged. He had left New Salem. They had written. The correspondence lagged, the letters stopped. Three years had passed. Ann and Abe became engaged.

As Lincoln and Ann made happy plans for their marriage, she was stricken with a swift and fatal illness. After she had gone, he was utterly desolate, inconsolable—for a while deranged with grief.

People believed that it was the memory of Ann Rutledge that shadowed the strange gloom in his haunted eyes. The remembrances of his mother, Nancy Hanks, of Ann Rutledge, of his young sister Sarah, were secrets that lay in the mysterious moods of despair that came and went but never wholly left the hidden sources of his nature.

II

A Lawyer in Springfield

"To this place, and the kindness of these people, I owe everything."

"Here I have lived a quarter of a century."

Joshua Speed's Store

IT WAS mid-April and the mud in the public square at Spring-field was deep, rich, and juicy. The traffic of the square kept it churned into a thick plastic soup. Horses, ox teams, droves of hogs, sheep, and cattle, and the heavy rawhide boots of its citizens made scrambled autobiographies across the square.

On this particular morning across the square rode long lean Abe Lincoln on his rawboned horse. It was not really his horse, for he had borrowed it to make the twenty-mile journey from New Salem.

He dismounted in front of Joshua Speed's general store, tied the horse to the hitching-post, and went in to see if Speed would trust him for the price of a bed and blankets. His saddlebags and his debts were all he owned. Instead, Speed offered to share his bedroom over the store with his gloomy friend. Abe took his saddlebags upstairs, looked at the big double bed, came down, and said with a grin, "Well, Speed, I'm moved."

In the chill evening, men who had business on the square dropped in and talked and argued before the fire in the back of Speed's store. There was Stephen Douglas, who was forging ahead so rapidly in the law and in politics. Abe and Douglas talked and argued by the cheery blaze and sized each other up. Speed's clerk was a young man with radical views named William Herndon. He shared the upstairs sleeping-quarters and made friends with Abe.

Abe spent his days in the law office that bore the sign "J. T. Stuart & A. Lincoln, Attorneys and Councillors at Law." When an election campaign got under way he was right in the thick of it, making speeches from stumps or the tail-ends of wagons, or wherever there was a crowd to listen. If he wasn't getting big law fees, he was never-theless well known and well liked by everybody. In politics young Abe called himself an Old Line Whig. People in Springfield were pretty evenly divided between Whigs and Democrats in 1837.

SPRINGFIELD was a booming town of over two thousand bustling people aiming to get ahead. There were high social goings-on. Abe was invited everywhere. At dances he would stand on the side lines and tell stories till there would be a group of laughing men around him. The girls wanting partners would look daggers at him.

Except one girl—the vivid, dominating girl from Kentucky who was visiting her sister, Mrs. Edwards. Mary Todd in the bloom of her twenty-two years was sure of herself. She was a proud and witty belle attracting the ambitious young politicians on the way to high places. She could pick and choose, but it was plain that Douglas and Lincoln were the favorites.

Billy Herndon, too, had won the favor of a dance. It was his first and last dance with Mary. "I engaged her for a waltz, and as we glided through it I fancied I never before had danced with a young lady who moved with such grace and ease. A few moments later, as we were promenading through the hall, I thought to compliment her graceful dancing by telling her that while I was conscious of my own awkward movements, she seemed to glide through the waltz with the ease of a serpent. The strange comparison was as unfortunate as it was hideous. I saw it in an instant, but too late to recall it. She halted for a moment, drew back, and her eyes flashed as she retorted: 'Mr. Herndon, comparison to a serpent is rather severe irony, especially to a newcomer.' " Billy had spilled the beans right at the start. A little grain of humor on each side might have saved a lifelong enmity.

When she was asked whom she would marry, "The one that has the best chance of being President," Mary flashed.

By some mysterious attraction of opposites, Mary Todd and Lincoln were drawn toward each other, fell in love, quarreled, made up, became engaged, quarreled again, and broke the engagement.

The powerful Edwards clan had given Mary a home in Springfield, though they now thought that Mary was making a poor choice of a husband in the backwoods lawyer who was so far below her social station.

The broken engagement would have settled it all, but a matchmaking friend appeared and invited the two to meet at her home. There was a reconciliation. Mary and Abe in a gay mood together wrote a political satire in the form of letters to a newspaper ridiculing a rival politician, James Shields, Democrat.

The Strange Duel — September 22, 1842

THESE letters, signed "Rebecca," appearing in the paper, had the whole town laughing at Mr. Shields's expense. Their broad ridicule enraged the fiery little Irishman Shields, who went to the paper demanding to know the author. When Mr. Lincoln, in order "to protect the ladies," said he was responsible, the furious Shields sent him a challenge to a duel. Mr. Lincoln, the well-known legislator, respectable citizen, and capable lawyer, who had got so many people out of scrapes, was now in a disgraceful scrape himself.

As the challenged party, he could choose the weapons. There was something splendid and fantastic about Lincoln's choice: cavalry broadswords! The two combatants were to stand and slash at each other on opposite sides of a ten-foot plank with long cavalry sabers.

When the news went round, the sporting bloods of Alton, Illinois, were all excitement. Men who wanted to see the fight were putting off in skiffs to the island in the Mississippi where the strange duel was to take place. The island was outside Illinois territory, so there would be no interference from state agents of the law.

When the crowd reached the island, Mr. Lincoln was found sitting on a log, running his thumb expertly along the edge of his long sword blade, as if it were his familiar ax. He rose slowly before the crowd to his full six foot four inches, lifted his long arm to its full stretch, and sliced little twigs off a limb high over his head, then sat down with a gleam in his eye.

Mr. Shields's friends look anxiously at their stocky, short-armed champion and hastily called a conference with Mr. Lincoln's seconds. After further discussion it was found that Mr. Lincoln had only written the letters for political effect, and not from any hard feelings against Mr. Shields personally. Mr. Shields's feelings were soothed and satisfied. The combatants shook hands, and were rowed back to the Illinois shore together in friendly confab. The Alton *Telegraph* gave them both a very severe editorial scolding. Lincoln was ashamed of the affair. Even long afterward, he would permit no one who valued his friendship to mention it.

"*Nothing new here excepting my marriage*"— *November* 4, 1842

BUT there was a savor of chivalry and romance to the scandalous affair that may have secretly pleased Mary Todd. For shortly the lovers were married in Springfield and went to live for a year at the Globe Tavern. They were very happy when their firstborn son arrived. They called him Robert.

Abe was now a responsible head of a family. Mary had ambitions. He had closed his partnership with Stuart and opened a law office with Stephen T. Logan in 1841. The Lincolns were looking for a home of their own, and finally bought the pleasant house at Eighth and Jackson streets that was to be their home in Springfield for many years.

In 1844, the partnership with Logan was dissolved and Lincoln asked his young friend Billy Herndon how he would like to come in as junior partner after he had passed his examination and had been admitted to the bar.

The Law Office — 1844

IT WAS a curious pair that sat at each end of the shabby green table each day in the dingy second-story office of Lincoln & Herndon. Billy Herndon was ten years Lincoln's junior. As they parked their feet high on the office furniture and talked of law cases or politics, Billy silently tried to fathom the secrets behind the gloomy face and cavernous eyes of his senior partner. Billy liked to read faces, and tried to guess what was beneath the dark melancholy and the sudden hilarious laughter of this peculiarsome man.

For the long bony sad man that was Billy's partner, the law office became a sanctuary and a refuge and a workshop, where through the years he slowly grew and learned and thought out the dark meanings and drifts of a troubled time. The law office was a world apart from the home on Eighth Street which he shared with Mary Todd, where they tried to compromise and adjust the strong tides and currents of their different natures, where their four sons were born, and three grew up into turbulent undisciplined youngsters.

Faithful Mary was determined that Abe should succeed and rise. She was always behind his plans and ambitions. Loyal Mary, with her wild rages and bitter remorses, wanted so fiercely that Abe should become successful and famous and sit in high places.

It was natural that they should think and plan for Congress and Washington. Many young lawyers who were in politics were aiming for election to Congress. The Whigs took turns at the nomination, and helped each other to get elected. "If anybody says I don't want to go to Congress they are badly mistaken," Abe wrote to a friend.

The Whigs nominated Abe to run against the Democratic candidate, Peter Cartwright, the fire-eating circuit rider and pioneer Methodist minister. Lincoln put all his untiring will to win into stump speeches, letters to editors, and appeals to friends. When old Peter spotted Abe just about to leave one of his meetings, he sang out,

"Lincoln, if you are not going to heaven, where are you going?"
"I'm going to Congress," spoke up Abe.

And after the votes had been counted, he went, with a big majority.

In Congress — 1847-1849

THE Lincolns were going to Washington, the whole family, including Robert, age four, and Baby Eddie, eighteen months old. There was all the excitement of getting ready and the send-off and good-by. There was the stop-off at Lexington, Kentucky, to visit the relatives, and the adventure of the long journey to the East and Washington.

Then came the big thrill and surprise of seeing Washington for the first time, the vast cobblestoned emptiness of Pennsylvania Avenue with the great temple of the Capitol at one end, and the gracious White House, the awesome Executive Mansion, at the other.

Abe soon fitted into the ways of Congress, learning the ropes and his way about in the House of Representatives. After all he was an old hand at political dealings and maneuvers. He had learned about back-scratching, logrolling and pork barrels, and political deals with the Long Nine in the Vandalia legislature. It was not long before the snobbish political cliques of Capitol Hill took him into their inner circles. You simply could not make an outsider of a man who could tell stories like that.

Senator Douglas of Illinois condescended to remember him. Douglas even remembered that they had been in the Illinois Legislature together. At New Salem, in Springfield, in Washington, wherever there was politics, Abe was at home. Now he belonged in the halls of Congress.

As he listened to the debate and argument in the House of Representatives he became aware of a theme that was at the back of all men's minds: slavery. There were Slave States, and Free States, two worlds, each striving fiercely for advantage, power, and control of the Government. West of the Mississippi the country was filling up, taking political form and shape, first in Territories and then coming into the Union as Free or Slave States. The two Senators from each new state might swing the balance of power to one side or the other in Congress.

The free North and the slave South were striving for control of the great Western lands. Abe soon found that slavery was not just an abstract question in the District of Columbia. Walking down the Avenue, Lincoln saw gangs of black men and women, sometimes chained together, going and coming from the slave market just south of Pennsylvania Avenue in sight of the national Capitol. He remembered the auction block at New Orleans when he was a boy of seventeen. Slave-dealing was a legitimate business for the great planters of Virginia and Maryland, but there were men from New England who raged at the sight of slave gangs going and coming on the streets of the nation's capital.

Before Lincoln had arrived in Washington, President Polk had declared war on Mexico. Lincoln opposed this land-grabbing war as a move of the Democratic party to gain more slave territory. He made a speech in Congress challenging the Government to prove whether the spot where the first blood of the war had been shed was on Mexican or United States territory. Back in Illinois the war was popular, and the state was supporting it with men and money, Lincoln's honest convictions about the "Spot Resolutions" killed any chance for his re-election in Illinois.

When the Whigs in Washington wanted to send a good speaker to New England to work for the election of old Zack Taylor, Lincoln was asked to go. Out in Illinois folks looked down on Yankees, but Abe's heart must have beat faster on Boston Common when he trod the same ground where the heroes of the Revolution had

walked, the men he had read about in his beloved *Life of Washington* by Parson Weems.

In Boston he spoke on the same platform with the great Whig-party leader William H. Seward, whose speeches he listened to with admiration. Lincoln made some good speeches in New England, and at Worcester they liked his plain talk and wanted him to come back and make more speeches like that. But when he went back to Springfield, Illinois, people were angry over his "Spot Resolutions" and gave him the cold shoulder.

During his second winter in Congress, he worked on a bill to restrict slavery in the District of Columbia, but it did not go through.

March the fourth, 1849, came, and his term was up. He hoped for, and had tried to land, an appointment for himself in Washington, but his saving angel said no. He came back to Springfield, to Mary Todd and the children, who had returned to the home on Eighth Street. It was all over. He was out of politics. But in the two years on Capitol Hill he had grown immensely, watching men of power in action, and himself learning to take a real part in the running of the whole United States of America. He had felt and seen the forces and tides that were pulling and rising and rushing on toward a dark future.

He was out of politics. "My future is behind me," he said. So he came back to Springfield and the dingy law office where faithful Billy Herndon had kept watch on the political fences as best he could while Abe had been away. He came back to the law, the deeds and the mortgages, and the rural quarrels and scrapes, to the dingy office that was a refuge and a workshop, where he could spill out on the old sofa and put his feet on the chairs and read the newspapers or installments of *Uncle Tom's Cabin* in the *National Era*, or sit in silence at the green table where Billy again watched and guessed at the moods and thoughts that gloomed in the deep sockets of his drooping gray eyes.

61

As he swung to and from the home and the office in his stooping plowman's stride, neighbors peered from behind curtains, wondered and shook their heads and smiled at the familiar figure, the tall scarecrow in the old high hat and the gray shawl.

Billy Herndon Paints a Portrait — 1850

"HE WAS so good and so odd a man, how in the hell could I help study him," said Herndon. Billy Herndon sat in their bleak second-story law office on the public square in Springfield watching and listening to his peculiar partner through the days that drifted into months and the months that passed into years. Billy could describe with affectionate detail the eccentricities of his senior partner as he saw him in the small happenings of the daily routine.

"When he got to the office, about 9 o'clock in the morning, the very first thing he did was to pick up a newspaper and read it aloud, much to my discomfort; he would spread himself out on the sofa. one leg on a chair, and the other on the table or stove.

"I have often said to Lincoln, 'Why do you always read aloud?' and to which he said: 'When I read aloud my two senses catch the idea. First, I see what I am reading, and secondly, I hear it read, and I can thus remember what I read the better.'

"Sometimes Lincoln would read something in the papers and that would suggest to him an idea and he would say: 'That puts me in mind of a story I heard down in Egypt in Illinois'; and then he would tell the story, and that story would suggest another, and so on. Nothing was done that morning. Declarations, briefs, pleas, demurrers, were flung to the winds. It was useless to attempt to read any more that morning.

"Mr. Lincoln, in his abstractions or in his misery, *seemed* to me to be a little bit off, so odd was he, and yet I know that for the time being he was in the lone land of his greatest thoughts. It has been

said of Mr. Lincoln that he was a many-sided man and, if he was, he certainly was a many-mooded man. I can see Lincoln now in my mind looking sad and grim, sitting at our table, pen in hand, while his chin rested in his left hand, his elbow resting on the table, he gazing in the distance all the while. There is a sad picture for you truly."

Though Herndon and Mrs. Lincoln had a strong dislike for each other, they both knew that living with Lincoln was about as comfortable as living with a slightly cracked and irresponsible good-natured bear.

If Herndon and Mrs. Lincoln disliked each other, there were reasons why. Lincoln and Billy split fifty-fifty the earnings of their law practice, but when Herndon had a political job on the side he did not share the proceeds with his partner. Billy had his shortcomings and irregularities and perhaps was not always an asset as a law partner.

After listening to his stories in a country store or on a street corner, people thought they knew all there was to simple Honest Abe. But Herndon knew better. He sensed the deep secret nature of this complex man who never revealed himself. There were high sunny hilltops and unsounded depths of gloom at which he could only guess and wonder.

"In our office on the west side of the square we had a long office table running north and south. Lincoln always took his seat on the east side of the table, looking westward, and I sat on the west side of the table, looking eastward, and thus we sat face to face. About one o'clock in the day the sun, especially in the summer, streamed through the western windows of our office and flooded Mr. Lincoln's face, so that I could see to the very back part of his eyes. When thus situated and in one of his abstract moods I studied the man and I think I could read his thoughts clearly, distinctly, certainly in a general way. On looking at the man thus, under the above conditions, speculatively, critically, he would to the observer's surprise, without warning, burst out in a loud laugh, or quickly spring up and run downstairs as if his house were on fire, saying nothing."

Circuit Lawyer — 1850

EIGHTEEN-FIFTY was a year for remembrance in the life of the little family in the house on Eighth Street.

Life and death opened and closed their mysterious portals for the Lincolns in grief and gladness. Four-year-old Edward died in February, and in December of the same year a new arrival came to gladden with new life the happy Christmas time. They called him William Wallace.

At the office clients came and went. Seeds from the free packages Congressmen gave their clients sifted out of the old secretary in the corner of the office and sprouted out of the dusty floor. Innumerable deeds and mortgages were signed on the stained green tablecloth.

In the familiar courtrooms Abe had shrewd ways and twists of argument to persuade juries. He won verdicts that saved the friendless and the frightened from human wolfishness. At a sensational murder trial when he defended the accused, Mr. Lincoln produced the murdered victim alive. He hadn't been murdered at all.

He could use a quick wit or emotional appeal or cold logic to suit the particular case and swing the jury to his side. Old Abe saved more than one friendless woman or scared farm hand from the shadow of the penitentiary or from the gallows. The stories of his cases were a saga of stark and comic human drama, the reality more fantastic than the rich humanity of his grotesque stories and fables.

There were long weeks and months away from home riding from town to town where the circuit courts were held. The journeys in the Eighth Circuit were an Illinois Odyssey, a prairie Canterbury Pilgrimage. In shabby boardinghouses, in dismal taverns, he sat among "the boys" and exchanged uproarious yarns from the inexhaustible collection he had stored through the years. Far into the night the smoky rafters rang with the blasts of laughter. Famous storytellers matched each other for the tallest tale until the fun waxed furious and the exhausted judges held their aching sides and begged the battling heroes to call it a draw. In the circuit towns boys played hooky to attend trials when they heard Abe was to plead.

Again, his mood would change to silent misery and he seemed to be lost in subterranean gloom. Somewhere in his spirit there always echoed the haunting refrain of a dismal ballad: "Oh, why should the spirit of mortal be proud?" He was a prairie Don Quixote, riding a bony Rosinante down a miry road at monstrous windmills of solemn sham, and the sharp lance of his curious wit smote mightily the pompous ogres of puff and pretense.

Back at the Springfield home he would try to compensate for his careless habits and absent-mindedness by letting Mary have her imperious way, and absorbing the fury of her storms with a vast patience. He smiled at the outrageous pranks of Willie and Bob with a large indulgence. Sometimes he would bring the precious pair with him to the office, where their antics tormented the long-suffering soul of Billy Herndon and delighted their doting father.

"He, Lincoln, used to come down to our office on a Sunday when Mrs. Lincoln had gone to church, *to show her new bonnet*, leaving Lincoln to care for and attend to the children. Lincoln would turn Willie and Tad loose in our office, and they soon gutted the room, gutted the shelves of books, rifled the drawers, and riddled boxes, battered the points of my gold pens against the stairs, turned over the inkstands on the papers, scattered letters over the office, and danced over them and the like. I have felt many a time that I wanted to wring the necks of these brats and pitch them out of the windows, but out of respect for Lincoln and knowing that he was abstracted, I shut my mouth, bit my lips, and left for parts unknown."

Black Ivory and Red Gold

Down in the crowded public square at Springfield, Abe and Billy were talking with "Forty-Niners," wagoners with their families and goods bound for California in the great stream of thousands of gold-rushers, walking, riding, rolling on to golden California to pick fortunes in yellow nuggets out of the mountain streams and secret veins of the earth. California was filling up so fast with "Argonauts" (as the Forty-Niners were called) that sne would soon apply for statehood. Would she come in Slave or Free?

It was a momentous decision for the nation, because there were just fifteen Slave and fifteen Free States represented in the United States Senate, and the two new Senators from California would throw the balance of power to one side or the other.

At the street corners Abe listened to the stories of the "underground railroad," of how the good gray Quakers along the northern shore of the Ohio waited to help runaway slaves who had crossed the river. Fugitive slaves were hidden in cellars, haystacks, and attics, and then passed secretly north at night to the next station until they reached free Canada and safety. The Fugitive Slave Law had just been passed and Southern slaveowners could claim their runaway slaves in Northern courts and have them brought back by Federal officers. Anyone helping a runaway slave was liable to prosecution by the owner, and a fine of $1000. In 1852 people were reading a new book called *Uncle Tom's Cabin*. It told of brutal overseers of bloodhounds pursuing slaves across the icy Ohio.

To appease the North for the hated Fugitive Slave Law, California was admitted to the Union as a Free State. This was called the Compromise of 1850. It upheld the old Missouri Compromise by which, thirty years before, Congress had established a line between the Northern Free States and the Southern Slave States. Lincoln believed the Missouri Compromise would solve the slavery question in time, and slavery would die out through education or the freeing of the slaves by government purchase.

The old order was changing. In 1852 solemn bells tolled throughout the land, the passing of Daniel Webster, the old Lion of the Constitution, and of Henry Clay, the great Pacificator. For decades these two had fought nobly to hold the Union together by tolerance and compromise. Lincoln admired these men. He had called himself in politics a "Clay man."

On March fourth, 1853, a new President was inaugurated in Washington. Franklin Pierce was the fourteenth President of the United States. People in the North were uneasy because although Pierce was a Northern Democrat, it was known that he had strong Southern sympathies.

One morning early in April, Lincoln burst into the law office, gay with the tidings of a new arrival in the Lincoln family. It was another boy. Officially his name was Thomas, but he grew up answering to the name of "Tad," abbreviated affectionately from "Tadpole." On Tad's first birthday, Billy Herndon was elected Mayor of Springfield.

So the turning years brought Presidents, Mayors, and Tadpoles, and out of the wet loam of the Illinois prairie, the armies of the returning corn thrust up in long green rows.

Abe Takes His Feet from the Table — 1854

IN THE obscure Springfield law office the partners sat with their feet on the windowsill, reading the papers that came in from the four corners of the Union. "Newspapers were his food, and politics his religion," said Billy. They were studying and discussing the slavery question, and the swift movement of events, trying to sound out the shape of circumstances and underlying principles dividing the country. In his gloomy moods Lincoln felt that he was out of politics for good, and thought of himself as an old man, politically finished. He would always be an unknown country lawyer.

He was reading in the papers a lot about Stephen A. Douglas, and he remembered how they had argued before the fire in the back of Speed's store, and how he had taken the measure of the man when they had been in the Illinois Legislature. He remembered how he had laughed at the vivacious young men pirouetting down the table at the Vandalia banquet, and the crashing crockery.

The colorful Douglas had risen rapidly in politics and in the law, to state and national office. In the United States Senate he now held the important position of chairman of the Committee on States and Territories, and was one of the most powerful national party leaders. Abe too had gone to Congress, but had come back, a political has-been, to the drudgery of a shabby law office.

Judge Douglas was shaking the country with a brand-new political doctrine which he said would solve the slavery question. A vast chunk of Western prairie beyond the Mississippi was opening up for settlement, railroads, enterprise, huge business empire and political power. Judge Douglas believed the future of American enterprise was in the West. He introduced a bill organizing this land into the Territories of Kansas and Nebraska. The bill provided that the slavery question in the new Territories should be decided by the votes of the local inhabitants instead of by the United States Congress. This was what he called Popular Sovereignty. When, through Douglas's efforts, the Kansas-Nebraska Bill passed the Congress and was signed by President Pierce, it meant that the old Missouri Compromise which Lincoln and many Northerners believed had settled the slavery question was at an end. Armed bands of immigrants were starting for Kansas from North and South, in a race to decide whether Kansas should be Slave or Free.

In the North the newspapers raved and famous clergymen held meetings. William Lloyd Garrison and the Abolitionists burned the

Constitution in public because it provided for the Fugitive Slave Law. Judge Douglas was burned in effigy in public squares. Ohio women sent him thirty pieces of silver in reminder of Judas. When he came to Chicago to speak for "squatter sovereignty," as it was contemptuously called, a furious mob howled outside his window till midnight. The angry Judge had to give up his speech.

But as popular indignation began to die down, the powerful Democratic party rallied behind the vivid Senator again. The newspapers were full of Douglas's announced intention to come to the great Illinois State Fair at Springfield to whip his Democratic following into line with his dramatic oratory.

The Kansas-Nebraska Bill was a challenge to Lincoln, rousing him to grapple with new problems. With the passing of the old Missouri Compromise and the world of Webster and Clay, all the securities of the America Lincoln had known were wiped out. If slavery should spread over the whole land, the Declaration of Independence and the Constitution would no longer stand, and in the end freedom would have no meaning for Black or White. If slavery was not wrong, then nothing was wrong. He must fight this evil thing with all he had and was. He must make the people see and understand the danger. Then the whole people would decide, and in the end the people were always right.

There comes a time when all the unrelated events fall into a pattern, the shapeless years take form, all the little rivers flow into one great stream of purpose. "To this end was I born, and for this cause came I into the world, that I should bear witness unto the truth."

As he slowly thought, analyzing the meaning of the time, its past and future, he was reborn and dedicated to a new vision of freedom and right.

Mr. Lincoln, sprawling by the office window, threw down the crumpled newspaper. Very slowly he heaved his great feet from their accustomed roost on the green table top. He rose, unbending his long body like a folding rule. He stretched his long arms above his head. It was an appallingly long stretch. It was the way he had stretched when he had held a cavalry saber waiting for a go at Mr. Shields. So Judge Douglas was coming to Springfield again. Old Abe was going to listen carefully to the great man's arguments for Popular Sovereignty, and he had made up his mind to answer them.

Illinois State Fair — October 4, 1854

It was October, and the great annual Illinois State Fair had brought thousands of visitors to Springfield from the surrounding counties. There was a smell of cattle, there were the parades and show-offs of prize ox teams, wide-haunched stallions, incredibly woolly sheep, complacent hogs of colossal size, and the clamorous hurly-burly of marvels, monsters, jugglers, mountebanks, fortune-tellers, bunco men, and common rogues. It was the great festival week of the year in Illinois. But the chief event was a political contest to be held in the State House, where both the Democratic champion, Judge Stephen Douglas, and Old Abe Lincoln were to speak on the Kansas-Nebraska Bill and Popular Sovereignty. The people were to be the judges.

Audiences in Illinois were the world's toughest, most tireless long-distance listeners. For three hours through the afternoon they listened to the thunder of the "Little Giant" on the virtues of Popular Sovereignty. "Let the people rule" was going to be a tough proposition for Mr. Lincoln to answer.

On the next afternoon Lincoln delivered his reply. He began his cool, clear argument, analyzed the history of the Missouri Compromise and the motives of the Declaration of Independence and the Constitution, justified the Compromise of 1850, saluted Jefferson and his great act in freeing the Northwest Territory forever of slavery, and bitterly denounced slavery and slave-owning.

In answer to Douglas's "the sacred right of self-government should be granted to each state," Lincoln replied; "The doctrine of self-government is right—absolutely and eternally right—but it has no just application as here attempted." It depended on "whether a negro is not or is a man. But if the negro is a man, is it not to that extent a total destruction of self-government to say that he too shall not govern himself?"

He spoke in plain language that people could understand. A noble style of language and powerful logic glowed in the words: "Stand with anybody that stands right. Stand with him while he is right, and part with him when he goes wrong. Stand with the Abolitionist in restoring the Missouri Compromise, and stand against him when he attempts to repeal the fugitive-slave law. In both cases you are right. In both cases you expose the dangerous extremes. In both you stand on middle ground, and hold the ship level and steady."

The speech was clear and simply expressed and was rich and vivid in thought and ideas. It was something new and different from the usual flowery political oratory of the day.

People left the State House thinking that they had heard a man in Springfield who could stand up to the Little Giant.

"The house approved the glorious triumph of truth by loud and continued huzzahs. The Nebraska Bill was shivered and like a tree of the forest was torn and rent asunder by the hot bolts of truth," wrote Billy Herndon in an ecstasy of enthusiasm for his hero. Twelve days later Douglas and Lincoln repeated their addresses at Peoria, and the first of Lincoln's great speeches became known as the Peoria address.

If politics was his life, as Herndon said, Lincoln had been resurrected. The anti-Nebraska party was waxing strong in Illinois. Lincoln was anxious to get into the thick of the battle again. He hoped that the friends in the Illinois Legislature would elect him United States Senator. When he saw this would not happen, he threw his influence to help elect a Democrat who was anti-Nebraska, although he himself was an Old Line Whig. Abe was beaten again. He was not discouraged; fired with a new determination to fight the spread of slavery, he went back to the law office, where his growing reputation was bringing him fat cases.

"Don't be so hard on the railroads, Billy," said Lincoln, showing Billy a draft for $4800. And then he explained how he had won a case for the railroad but had to sue his client to collect his fee. He won both cases.

Though he still worked conscientiously on law cases, he was deeply pondering the slavery question and the Nebraska Bill, and where he must stand in the terrible struggle between the North and the South that seemed to be drawing nearer. The North and the South were sending parties of settlers to Kansas to settle the slavery question by Popular Sovereignty. Lincoln was reading in the papers of savage dramas.

In the West over Kansas black smoke and flame were rising against a red sky. A drunken band of Missouri Border Ruffians had crossed into Kansas and burned and sacked the town of Lawrence. Three days later Osawatomie Brown and his sons had taken a midnight vengeance on five men whom they murdered in cold blood. Fierce passions were driving men to terrible deeds.

Lincoln's ship, held "level and steady," was rocking on dark and violent waters. The image of savage Old John Brown, with his madman's eyes, against the smoke of a burning town, haunted men's minds to the refrain of a bitter chant—"Kansas, Bleeding Kansas."

Black Republicans — 1856

ANTI-NEBRASKA Democrats, Whigs, and Abolitionists were pouring into Bloomington, Illinois, late in May 1856, to take part in the big convention of the newly formed Republican party to elect delegates to a state convention. Herndon was there helping get things organized. He was in trouble because he had put Lincoln's name down with those who had called the convention and Lincoln's conservative friends were objecting to this unauthorized procedure. Billy telegraphed Lincoln telling him what he had done. "All right. Go ahead. Will meet you radicals and all. A. Lincoln," came the answer. Lincoln had made his great decision.

When the convention got under way at Mason's Hall over Humphrey's Cheap Store, Abe was there on the platform. It meant a lot to the new party to have an Old Line Whig of Lincoln's standing with them. There were calls for a speech. Lincoln came forward and began to speak. Reporters who started to take down his words forgot to use their pencils. He was breathing the breath of life and soul into the newborn party. "He stood before the throne of Eternal Right, and unburdened his penitential and inspired soul. If Mr. Lincoln was six feet four inches usually, at Bloomington he was seven feet," wrote the enraptured Billy.

"While, in all probability, no resort to force will be needed, our moderation and forbearance will stand us in good stead, when, if ever, WE MUST MAKE AN APPEAL TO BATTLE AND TO THE GOD OF HOSTS!" Lincoln prophesied, as he closed his speech. Just before, he had said, "We must make this a land of liberty in fact, as it is in name. WE SHALL SAY TO THE SOUTHERN DISUNIONISTS, 'WE WON'T GO OUT OF THE UNION AND YOU SHAN'T!!!' "

The grandeur of the speech was talked of by those who heard it until it became a legend. Because no word of it was recorded by newspapermen, it became known by the romantic name of the "Lost Speech." People left the hall that night saying "It's the best speech ever made in Illinois, and it puts Lincoln in line for the Presidency."

In Springfield, five nights later, a mass meeting was called to ratify the Bloomington convention. When Mr. Lincoln and Billy showed up at the meeting, there was one other Republican there, and no one else at all. "It was more than I expected," remarked Lincoln, and added hopefully, "Though all seems dead, be hopeful. Let us adjourn and appeal to the people."

After the Lost Speech, people began looking to Lincoln as the foremost Republican in Illinois. He got letters from all over the state, and Indiana as well, asking him to speak. People wanted to hear what Abe had to say about it.

When the Republican party held its first national convention and nominated John C. Frémont, Lincoln's name received 110 votes for the Vice-Presidency, but he was not nominated. Votes for him showed that people were thinking of him as capable for high office. Back in central Illinois Abe was working with all his might to organize the rising young Republican party. He made fifty speeches in the campaign for Frémont. Frémont and the Republicans were defeated; Buchanan, the Democratic candidate, was elected. Buchanan was soon looked upon as a weak tool of the South.

The young Republicans were not discouraged. Although defeated, they knew that their strength was growing rapidly throughout the country. They would work and wait for another chance. Lincoln made a rousing address before the Republican leaders at a banquet in Chicago. When he spoke of Liberty and Principle, people listened spellbound to the power of his words.

He was the most prominent figure in the Republican party in the state. He was the tallest man in Illinois.

The Negro Is a Man — March 6, 1857

Two DAYS after Buchanan's inauguration, the Supreme Court announced its Dred Scott decision, ruling that a Negro was not a citizen of the United States, but the property and chattel of his owner, and that the Missouri Compromise had been invalid from its inception. The Southern slaveholders now seemed all-powerful.

76

They controlled the Congress, the Chief Executive, and now the Supreme Court. The Dred Scott decision made it possible for slavery to be carried into the Free States and spread all over the Union. Abolition extremists were so angry that they proposed that the Free States secede from the Union.

Douglas, the Democratic Senator from Illinois, was coming to Springfield to use all his power and prestige to defend the Dred Scott decision and to proclaim his remedy for all difficulties, "Popular Sovereignty." Lincoln sat in the familiar Hall of Representatives and listened to the Little Giant's thunder, and took the measure of his gaudy, shifting mind. Douglas argued that the Declaration of Independence applied only to white men and did not include Negroes, and urged obedience to the Supreme Court as a patriotic duty.

Two weeks later, in the same place, Lincoln spoke in reply to Douglas. He said: "In those days our Declaration of Independence was held sacred by all, and thought to include all; but now, to aid in making the bondage of the negro universal and eternal, it is assailed and sneered at and construed, and hawked at and torn, till, if its framers could rise from their graves, they could not at all recognize it. All the powers of earth seem rapidly combining against him. Mammon is after him, ambition follows, philosophy follows, and the theology of the day is fast joining the cry."

"We think the Dred Scott decision is erroneous. We know the court that made it has often overruled its own decisions, and we shall do what we can to have it to overrule this."

He summed up in swift and sharp sentences the meaning of the two opposing parties. "The Republicans inculcate, with whatever of ability they can, that the negro is a man, that his bondage is cruelly wrong, and that the field of his oppression ought not to be enlarged.

"The Democrats deny his manhood; deny, or dwarf to insignificance, the wrong of his bondage; so far as possible, crush all sympathy for him, and cultivate and excite hatred and disgust against him; compliment themselves as Union-savers for doing so, and call the indefinite outspreading of his bondage 'a sacred right of self-government.' "

Lincoln's neighbors in Springfield were astonished. What had happened to the eccentric lawyer, the absent-minded failure they had passed daily on the streets for twenty years, that he could stand up to a great national leader like Douglas? How ever could Old Abe make a great speech like that?

The Stovepipe Hat — 1858

THE Republican politicians around Springfield were thinking that Abe Lincoln was the only man who could stand up against the Judge in the coming election for United States Senator from Illinois. Judge Douglas was coming back from Capitol Hill to campaign for himself and "the great Pur-in-ci-pull of Popular Sovereignty." The Democratic party had nominated him and were going to give him a big send-off for victory.

Everybody knew that Abe was ready and willing to accept the Republican nomination. He had said that all "Popular Sovereignty" meant was that "if any one man choose to enslave another, no third man shall be allowed to object." This was something for the Judge to put in his pipe.

For some weeks Herndon had noticed that his partner had been making notes on scraps of paper and envelopes and stowing them away in the lining of his stovepipe hat. In the hat he carried his unanswered letters, his bank account, his big red handkerchief, and reminders. When he had delivered letters in New Salem he had learned to keep things under his hat. It was a secret closet, a little storehouse, a handy attic for things to remember, where he could keep and always find them.

One morning Lincoln came into the office and took from the

stovepipe hat the scraps and notes all pasted together. "Billy," he said, "I want now to read my speech, and after I am done, I want your opinion of it in all directions." Billy was delighted and Abe hoisted his feet to the table and read as Billy listened.

"If we could first know where we are, and whither we are tending, we could better judge what to do, and how to do it. We are now far into the fifth year since a policy was initiated with the avowed object and confident promise of putting an end to slavery agitation. Under the operation of that policy, that agitation has not only not ceased, but has constantly augmented. In my opinion, it will not cease until a crisis shall have been reached and passed. 'A house divided against itself cannot stand.' I believe this government cannot endure permanently half slave and half free. I do not expect the Union to be dissolved—I do not expect the house to fall—but I do expect that it will cease to be divided. It will become all one thing, or all the other. Either the opponents of slavery will arrest the further spread of it, and place it where the public mind shall rest in the belief that it is in the course of ultimate extinction; or its advocates will push it forward till it shall become alike lawful in all the States, old as well as new, North as well as South."

When he had finished, he looked quietly at Billy from under heavy brows. Billy waited, taming wild processions of hosannahs, and then said in his best legal manner: "The speech is a good one, written with great power, and will bring you prominently before the American people. It is in advance of the age, but deliver it just as you have written it." Then jumping to his feet with a face of prophecy, he flashed, "Lincoln, deliver and publish your speech just as you have written it; it will make you President of the United States."

Lincoln took the speech over to the State House and read it to the bosses. They didn't like it at all. "Take out that about the House Divided. People won't like it," the politicians said. When Lincoln read the speech to the convention, not a word had been changed.

When the campaign was over and lost, the politicians came around in droves and said "We told you so." Lincoln supposed they would all desert him on account of the House Divided speech, but "there is one man that will stick by me to the end. He understands it and its importance, and that man is Billy Herndon, my good old and tried friend."

When the winds of abuse blew strong, he wrote, "If I had to draw a pen across my record and erase my whole life from sight, and I had one poor gift or choice left as to what I should save from the wreck, I should choose that speech and leave it to the world un-erased."

The Tall Sucker and the Little Giant — 1858

"RESOLVED, that Abraham Lincoln is the first and only choice of the Republicans of Illinois for the United States Senate as the successor of Stephen A. Douglas."

The State Convention had unanimously adopted the resolution, and Lincoln had accepted in his House Divided speech. He had answered the Judge's first speech at Chicago, and replied to his speech in Springfield, but his friends were clamoring for a debate, an all-out fight with the Judge in the form of a series of debates right on the same platform. Judge Douglas replied magnanimously to Lincoln's challenge note, and the terms were arranged. Really the Judge was not happy about it. He was a nationally famous man and had everything to lose and very little to gain in a contest with the lawyer who was hardly known outside his own state.

Politics were a gorgeous let-off and blow-up that brought color and excitement to drab rural towns and monotonous days on lonely farms. There would be roaring parades, waving banners, and crashing bands, with corn likker and tobacco juice flowing wild and free.

There were to be seven joint debates in mushroom towns throughout the state. The Little Giant would thunder his fireworks and the Tall Sucker would come back with his tough close-reasoned arguments alternately as they moved from town to town. It was an Illinois holiday, with all the excitement and drama of a personal encounter. It was a frontier free-for-all which delighted leather-necked horse-and-alligator men.

The first debate was in the northern town of Ottawa. On Saturday morning thousands of people were milling around the platform in the center of the public square. The August sun burned down on boisterous parades marching through clouds of yellow dust. Competing bands tried to drown each other out with blaring horns and thumping drums. Two cannon roared to announce the arrival of the Judge; Lincoln's lanky frame was recognized towering above the crowd. The short stout figure of the Judge stepped forward on the platform and his deep voice boomed across the square. The battle was on.

Papers spread the speeches all over the country with violently partisan reports. When Douglas accused Lincoln of having attended an Abolitionist meeting and this was proved untrue, the papers made it hot for the Judge. He telegraphed a friend: "The hell hounds are on my track. For God's sake, Linder, come and help me fight them." The telegram got into the Republican papers, and "For-God's-Sake-Linder" added to the fun.

The next debate was at Freeport a week later. It was Lincoln's turn to speak first and the crowd was with him. He answered shrewdly a list of tricky questions the Judge had hurled at him. Abe then asked some questions of Douglas. The Judge's answer lost him the support of many Southern Democrats later, as Lincoln had intended it should.

The third debate was "down in Egypt," at Jonesboro, a town in the southern, proslavery end of Illinois. Here Lincoln's antislavery

views were unpopular and Douglas had the advantage. The Judge got personal and said that Lincoln had had to be carried off the platform after the Ottawa debate, which was true, but it was on the shoulders of enthusiastic admirers.

The next round was at Charleston near the Indiana border, where Lincoln had many old friends and was welcomed with a huge banner depicting him with a pioneer wagon.

October had come with rain and a cold wind blowing through Galesburg when the debaters arrived there. This was Republican territory. There was a crowd of antislavery farmers and laborers. A sign read, "Small Fisted Farmers, Mud Sills of Society, Greasy Mechanics for A. Lincoln," and Abe spoke in front of a huge sign with the encouraging words "Knox College for Lincoln." He spoke on his favorite theme, the Declaration of Independence. When it declared all men to be created free and equal, it included the Negro. He defied the Judge to prove that the Fathers had not intended it so. He argued that slavery was wrong and replied to something Douglas had said—that he didn't himself "care whether slavery was voted up or down."

In spite of the brass cannon, the special trains, and the reception banquets, the going had been getting rougher for the Judge as the debates went on. Between the scheduled meetings the candidates spoke almost daily in the small towns in the vicinity, thus reaching many more than attended the formal debates. Lincoln rode modestly in a day coach or a freight train, and the Republicans hauled him into town in a hay wagon as an appeal to the working classes.

Papers all over the country were printing the Lincoln-Douglas debates and the whole nation was listening. Lincoln's old friends and enemies were asking questions. Was it possible that this clowning lawyer was going to the top, was becoming a national figure? Was it true that Old Abe was really a great man and had been all along and they never guessed it? Letters were coming to editors in Illinois from the East asking "Who is this man that is answering Douglas in your state? Do you realize that no greater speeches have been made on public questions in the history of this country, that his knowledge of these subjects is profound, his logic unanswerable, his style inimitable?" Well, they hadn't realized it yet, not back in Springfield.

Quincy was the largest town at which the champions were to meet. It was an important Illinois commercial center. The Republicans turned out in force, carrying at the head of the parade a live and bewildered raccoon on the top of a tall pole. This was the sign of the Old Line Whig party from which Abe had graduated. The Democrats derisively carried a dead raccoon hanging by the tail.

As the prairie wind tossed the dead leaves and the living speech across the square, Lincoln said: "I was aware, when it was first agreed that Judge Douglas and I were to have these seven joint discussions, that they were the successive acts of a drama—perhaps I should say, to be enacted not merely in the face of audiences like this, but in the face of the nation, and to some extent, by my relation to him, and not from anything in myself, in the face of the world; and I am anxious that they should be conducted with dignity and in the good temper which would be befitting the vast audience before which it was conducted."

He knew he was moving to the center of a stage on which the eyes of America were fixed.

Referring to the Judge's quarrel with the Buchanan Administration, Lincoln told the story of the pioneer wife watching a fight between her husband and a bear. She kept shouting: "Go it, husband; go it, bear!"

Abe and the Judge came down the Mississippi by boat to Alton for the final debate in the public square overlooking the great river. Perhaps Abe remembered that he had come to Alton once before to fight a prominent Democrat on an island in the river. In Alton, years before, a mob had brutally murdered the Abolitionist editor

Elijah Lovejoy. It was Democratic territory, and the small crowd was with the Judge, whose turn it was to have the first and last speech. He wound up with a brilliant résumé of the familiar arguments he had used so often.

In reply Lincoln made the clearest statement of his views during the whole debate, especially as to slavery. He summed up: "The sentiment that contemplates the institution of slavery in this country as a wrong is the sentiment of the Republican party. The Democratic policy in regard to that institution will not tolerate the merest breath, the slightest hint, of the least degree of wrong about it.

"That is the real issue. That is the issue that will continue in this country when these poor tongues of Judge Douglas and myself shall be silent. It is the eternal struggle between these two principles—right and wrong—throughout the world. They are the two principles that have stood face to face from the beginning of time; and will ever continue to struggle. The one is the common right of humanity, and the other the divine right of kings. It is the same principle in whatever shape it develops itself. It is the same spirit that says, 'You toil and work and earn bread, and I'll eat it.' No matter in what shape it comes, whether from the mouth of a king who seeks to bestride the people of his own nation and live by the fruit of their labor, or from one race of men as an apology for enslaving another race, it is the same tyrannical principle."

The dry leaves blew across the square overlooking the river. The seven debates were over. Back home in farmhouses, people were thinking over what this man Lincoln had said. People were saying, "We've either got to keep slavery back or it's going to spread all over the country. That's the real question that's behind all this. Lincoln is right." The people were beginning to understand.

Lincoln received 1600 more of the people's votes than Douglas, but Douglas was elected by the State Senate, which was strongly Democratic. At the time the State Senate and not the people elected the United States Senators. Lincoln had really won the election and lost the office.

After the terrific strain of the debates, Lincoln came back to the quiet Springfield office, lean and strong and more vital than before. He had grown tremendously in spiritual stature and he now had a national reputation. His speeches had been printed throughout the country and read by millions. The momentary gloom of defeat and reaction passed quickly. In the lull after battle were quiet months, and then in September a trip to Ohio to speak at Cincinnati and Columbus. Nearly a year had passed since the great debates, like a time of stillness before storm—but the lull was not for long.

Suddenly the telegraph wires were sending a wild alarm. For two days the nightmare of a slave rebellion hung over the land. John Brown, Osawatomie Brown, had captured the arsenal at Harper's Ferry and was going to lead a slave revolt on to Washington. For two days the wires were cut, severing Harper's Ferry from the world. Then news came through of the fight at the engine house, and the capture of a mad fanatic. Probably a Republican plot, the Democratic newspapers suggested. The charges against the party were serious, and called for denial by Republican leaders. Lincoln was silent about John Brown, sentenced to be hung in thirty days. Lincoln's legal mind abhorred deeds of violence and men acting without the law, but for the Abolitionists a new martyr-saint was enshrined in the Temple of Freedom.

John Brown's Body — 1859

"THIS is a beautiful country. I never had the pleasure of seeing it before," John Brown said wistfully, looking toward the blue mountain ranges.

The stern old Puritan with his white mane and flowing beard

sat on his coffin. Two white horses drew the lumbering wagon up to the scaffold. He stood serene and straight. He was dying with a halo of martyrdom. He knew how to die. He had written his last message on a scrap of paper.

"Charlestown, Va. 2 December, 1859

"I John Brown am now quite *certain* that the crimes of this *guilty land: will* never be purged *away;* but with Blood. I had *as I now think:* vainly flattered myself that without *very much* bloodshed; it might be done."[1]

Among the fifteen hundred troops standing solemnly around the scaffold was an officer named Thomas Jonathan Jackson and a militiaman named John Wilkes Booth.

The ax fell sharply on the hangman's rope, and John Brown's body swung between heaven and earth. Silence. In slow solemnity a voice said: "So perish all such enemies of Virginia! All such enemies of the Union! All such enemies of the human race!"

In Albany, New York, one hundred cannon boomed out in token of the passing of John Brown's soul.

Six weeks before, eighteen men in a covered wagon loaded with ammunition had crossed the railroad bridge into the little town under the heights above the juncture of the Potomac and Shenandoah rivers. Brown's raiders captured the United States arsenal in the town, and held out in the engine house against the local militia for a day and night. Marines under Colonel Robert E. Lee stormed the engine house and smashed in the doors. Osawatomie, with one hand on the pulse of his dying son and a rifle in the other, was beaten down and captured.

In the crowded courtroom in Charleston, eight miles away, Brown rose from his cot and addressed the court.

"I have, may it please the Court, a few words to say . . . Had I interfered in the manner which I admit, and which I admit has been

'O. G. Villard: *John Brown*

fairly proved—for I admire the truthfulness and candor of the greater portion of the witnesses who have testified in this case—had I so interfered in the behalf of the rich, the powerful, the intelligent, the so-called great, or in behalf of any of their friends, either father, mother, brother, sister, wife or children, or any of that class, and suffered and sacrificed what I have in this interference, it would have been all right. Every man in this Court would have deemed it an act worthy of reward rather than punishment.

"This Court acknowledges, too, as I suppose, the validity of the law of God. I see a book kissed, which I suppose to be the Bible, or at least the New Testament, which teaches me that all things whatsoever I would that men should do to me, I should do even so to them. It teaches me, further, to remember them that are in bonds as bound with them. I endeavored to act up to that instruction. I say I am yet too young to understand that God is any respecter of persons. I believe that to have interfered as I have done, as I have always freely admitted I have done, in behalf of His despised poor, I did no wrong, but right. Now, if it is deemed necessary that I should forfeit my life for the furtherance of the ends of justice, and mingle my blood further with the blood of my children and with the blood of millions in this slave country whose rights are disregarded by wicked, cruel and unjust enactments, I say let it be done."[1]

Thus John Brown to the court and to eternity in answer to the routine question why sentence should not be passed upon him.

After Brown's execution fevered meetings were held by sympathizers in great halls throughout the North. In Boston, Tremont Temple was crowded to the doors by a meeting "to witness John Brown's resurrection." Emerson wrote, "Nothing can resist the sympathy which all elevated minds must feel with Brown, and through them the whole civilised world." Lincoln's legal mind passing judgment in Kansas spoke his personal verdict: "Old John Brown

[1] O. G. Villard: *John Brown.*

has been executed for treason against a State. We cannot object, even though he agreed with us in thinking slavery wrong. That cannot excuse violence, bloodshed, and treason. It could avail him nothing that he might think himself right." The soul of old John Brown and his seven wild sons riding the night wind under a Kansas moon was a living legend and a marching song to raise up armies.

"Not much of me."— 1859

JESSE W. FELL of Bloomington was a promoter of big real-estate deals. He was a friend of Lincoln's and he liked to promote his friends. He had talked about him to important people in the East who had read Lincoln's speeches. "We have two giants in Illinois; Douglas is the little Giant, and Abe Lincoln is the big one," he told them.

He said to Lincoln that if people knew more about him he would have a good chance for the Presidency, to be the dark horse. Fell told Lincoln that the common people would like to know about him in a personal way, about his folks and where he came from. He asked Lincoln to write something about himself to give people the facts of his life.

Lincoln wrote Mr. Fell this letter:

"Springfield, December 20, 1859

"My Dear Sir: Herewith is a little sketch, as you requested. There is not much of it, for the reason, I suppose, that there is not much of me. If anything be made out of it I wish it to be modest, and not to go beyond the material. If it were thought necessary to incorporate anything from any of my speeches, I suppose there would be no objection. Of course it must not appear to have been written by myself.

"Yours very truly,

"A. LINCOLN

"I was born Feb. 12, 1809, in Hardin County, Kentucky. My parents were both born in Virginia, of undistinguished families—second families, perhaps I should say. My mother, who died in my tenth year, was of a family of the name of Hanks, some of whom now reside in Adams, and others in Macon County, Illinois. My paternal grandfather, Abraham Lincoln, emigrated from Rockingham County, Virginia, to Kentucky about 1781 or 1782, where a year or two later he was killed by the Indians, not in battle, but by stealth, when he was laboring to open a farm in the forest. His ancestors, who were Quakers, went to Virginia from Berks County, Pennsylvania. An effort to identify them with the New England family of the same name ended in nothing more definite than a similarity of Christian names in both families, such as Enoch, Levi, Mordecai, Solomon, Abraham, and the like.

"My father, at the death of his father, was but six years of age, and he grew up literally without education. He removed from Kentucky to what is now Spencer County, Indiana, in my eighth year. We reached our new home about the time the State came into the Union. It was a wild region, with many bears and other wild animals still in the woods. There I grew up. There were some schools, so called, but no qualification was ever required of a teacher beyond 'readin', writin', and cipherin' ' to the rule of three. If a straggler supposed to understand Latin happened to sojourn in the neighborhood, he was looked upon as a wizard. There was absolutely nothing to excite ambition for education. Of course, when I came of age I did not know much. Still, somehow, I could read, write, and cipher to the rule of three, but that was all. I have not been to school since. The little advance I now have upon this store of education, I have picked up from time to time under the pressure of necessity.

"I was raised to farm work, which I continued till I was twenty-two. At twenty-one I came to Illinois, Macon County. Then I got to New Salem, at that time in Sangamon, now in Menard County, where I remained a year as a sort of clerk in a store. Then came the Black Hawk war; and I was elected a captain of volunteers, a success which gave me more pleasure than any I have had since. I went the campaign, was elated, ran for the legislature the same year (1832), and was beaten—the only time I ever have been beaten by the people. The next and three succeeding biennial elections I was elected to the legislature. I was not a candidate afterward. During this legislative period I had studied law, and removed to Springfield to practise it. In 1846 I was once elected to the lower House of Congress. Was not a candidate for reëlection. From 1849 to 1854, both inclusive, practised law more assiduously than ever before. Always a Whig in politics; and generally on the Whig electoral tickets, making active canvasses. I was losing interest in politics when the repeal of the Missouri compromise aroused me again. What I have done since then is pretty well known.

"If any personal description of me is thought desirable, it may be said I am, in height, six feet four inches, nearly; lean in flesh, weighing on an average one hundred and eighty pounds; dark complexion, with coarse black hair and gray eyes. No other marks or brands recollected."

Cooper Union — February, 1860

AFTER the Douglas debates, Lincoln had come back to the law office and the practice, and faithful Billy Herndon. He did not mourn for long over personal defeat. Angry waters were sweeping away old barriers and houses founded on sand. Speaking at Columbus and Cincinnati, he hammered away at slavery. In February he took a train for New York, where he had been invited to speak. He had been working for weeks preparing the speech. He wanted to analyze difficult problems in politics, and answer doubts and questions about where the Republicans stood.

When he arrived in New York the committee took him to the Astor House. He was to speak at Cooper Union. A February blizzard blew fine snow around the big brownstone building at Eighth Street and Fourth Avenue. In the hall yellow gaslight shone on a forest of white pillars and a blur of fifteen hundred faces. On the platform sat the wise men of the East. The audience was called "distinguished."

The famous scholar and poet William Cullen Bryant introduced him. Abe unfolded his long six foot four and stepped forward. He was uncomfortable in his new tight shoes and black suit, all rumpled and creased. The New York sophisticates craned their necks around the pillars for their first look at the "Tall Sucker," the grotesque giant who had risen out of the tall corn and hammered down the arguments of the great Douglas with phrases that still burned in their memory.

As he spoke, slowly getting into his stride, his first awkwardness vanished. Soon he was speaking in the high-pitched voice with the soft Kentucky drawl.

He went back into the beginnings of the Constitution and showed how the Founding Fathers had never intended slavery should spread. "As those fathers marked it, so let it be again marked, as an evil not to be extended, but to be tolerated and protected only because of and so far as its actual presence among us makes that toleration and protection a necessity.

"And now, if they would listen—as I suppose they will not—I would address a few words to the Southern people."

He replied to Southern accusations that Republicanism was sectional, revolutionary, had stirred up the slavery question and insurrection among the slaves.

"John Brown was no Republican; and you have failed to implicate a single Republican in his Harper's Ferry enterprise. John Brown's effort was peculiar. It was not a slave insurrection. It was an attempt

94

by white men to get up a revolt among slaves, in which the slaves refused to participate. In fact, it was so absurd that the slaves, with all their ignorance, saw plainly enough it could not succeed."

He said of the Dred Scott decision "that it was mainly based upon a mistaken statement of fact—the statement in the opinion that 'the right of property in a slave is distinctly and expressly affirmed in the Constitution.' An inspection of the Constitution will show that the right of property in a slave is not 'distinctly and expressly affirmed' in it."

Further on, he simplified the whole stormy picture. To the Republicans he said: "Their thinking it right and our thinking it wrong is the precise fact upon which depends the whole controversy.

"Wrong as we think slavery is, we can yet afford to let it alone where it is, because that much is due to the necessity arising from its actual presence in the nation; but can we, while our votes will prevent it, allow it to spread into the national Territories, and to overrun us here in these free States? If our sense of duty forbids this, then let us stand by our duty fearlessly and effectively. Let us have faith that right makes might, and in that faith let us to the end dare to do our duty as we understand it."

It was over. Applause, cheers, hats thrown in the air, and congratulations. Lincoln took a dreary ride on a Broadway streetcar to the Astor House. The next morning he read in the newspaper about himself: "The tones, the gestures, the kindling eye and mirth-provoking look defy the reporter's skill. The vast assemblage frequently rang with shouts of applause. No man ever before made such an impression on his first appeal to a New York audience."

Not many people in New York bothered about whether Abe Lincoln would be a possible candidate for nomination at the Republican National Convention eight months ahead. They thought William H. Seward would be the most likely man for next President. But out in central Illinois important people like lawyers and newspaper editors had begun to talk about Old Abe as a pretty good possibility for the Republican candidate from Illinois.

The Rail-Splitter Candidate – May, 1860

IN MAY the Republican state convention met in Decatur to decide on their candidate for President at the National Convention. This was to be held in Chicago, where the Middle West would have a chance to make itself felt in national politics, and Illinois Republicans were planning to have something to say.

One day when Lincoln dropped into the crowded hall to see how things were going, there was a sudden rumpus started by the boisterous entrance of new delegates. It was old John Hanks, Lincoln's cousin, marching in with two long weather-beaten fence rails. Between the rails was a banner written in large letters:

ABRAHAM LINCOLN

THE RAIL CANDIDATE

FOR PRESIDENT IN 1860

TWO RAILS FROM ABOUT 3,000 MADE IN 1830

BY THOS. HANKS AND ABE LINCOLN—

WHOSE FATHER WAS THE FIRST PIONEER OF MACON COUNTY

There was a wild wave of whoops and cheers that swept the convention as the Macon County delegation, headed by old John Hanks, paraded around the hall. It was a dramatic surprise with an exuberant frontier thrill. There were shouts of "Lincoln, identify your work!" There was laughter and suspense as Abe carefully inspected the weathered rails and drawled, "I cannot say that I split these rails, but I have split a great many better-looking ones." There was an avalanche of cheers and yells for the Rail-Splitter candidate and more triumphal parades. The name stuck.

96

The Illinois delegates went off to Chicago, instructed to vote for the Rail-Splitter candidate at the Republican National Convention. The name had meaning along the Ohio Valley and on the prairie farms. It was a symbol that spoke to people who worked with their hands. It said "Here is your man."

Nominated – May 12, 1860

CHICAGO in 1860 was a city on stilts still climbing out of the lake-shore mud. But she was giving the Republican National Convention a windy Western welcome, mud and all. Delegates and political henchmen on excursion trains were pouring into the city by thousands for the big week, with banners, sashes, and high hats. Seward men, Chase men, Bates or Cameron men, and supporters of lesser candidates came in by cheering trainloads. William H. Seward, the old antislavery war-horse, was by far the most prominent and likely candidate.

The Convention Hall was a vast barnlike structure that could hold ten thousand people. It was called the Wigwam. Day and night the frenzied political bosses traded and swapped and persuaded among the excited delegates. Norman B. Judd, Lincoln's manager, had nailed Indiana and Pennsylvania for Lincoln. A terrific roar followed the nomination of Seward. But the Illinois captains had been gathering to the Wigwam armies of lusty Hog Callers, Illinois Suckers, and Indiana Hoosiers, who, when the signals were given, let out a blast as Lincoln was proposed that shook the Wigwam and roared over the prairie.

On the first ballot Seward led with 173½ votes, with Lincoln in second place with 102, and Cameron with 50. On the second ballot Cameron withdrew, giving his fifty votes to Lincoln. The score now stood Seward 184½ and Lincoln 181. The convention was wild with excitement over the dark horse from Illinois.

As the ballots were called on the third vote, the suspense grew tense. Two hundred and thirty-one and one-half for Lincoln—needing only 2 ½ more to give him the nomination.

A man in the Ohio delegation leaped on a chair and shouted, "Mr. Chairman, I rise to change four votes from Chase to Lincoln."

A moment of utter stillness and then an explosion of ten thousand terrific whoops. The Lincoln crowd went daft with joy. Venerable judges embraced, wept, danced, demolished silk hats. Cannon boomed, the frenzy spread over the city. Old Abe from Springfield was Republican candidate for the Presidency of the United States.

In Springfield, the day before the nomination, Lincoln had played handball with "the boys." The next day at the office of the *Illinois State Journal* he received calmly the telegram announcing his nomination. Friends swarmed around as he came down to the street. But he soon broke away saying "There is a little woman at our house who is more interested in this dispatch than I am."

That night all Illinois celebrated. In sleepy little prairie towns there were endless parades and singing marchers in torchlight processions. Burning tar barrels and rail fences lighted milling cornhuskers as they roared around the public squares.

In far-off Washington Senator Douglas was saying wistfully, "There won't be a tar barrel left in Illinois tonight."

Lincoln, in the front yard of the Springfield home, explained to a crowd of fifteen hundred serenaders clamoring for a speech, "The time comes upon every public man when it is best for him to keep his lips closed. That time has come upon me." To people who wanted him to talk politics he handed copies of his speeches. He had said his say, plainly and often. And he stood by just what he had said. He stayed at home, listened and smiled and told a story as the country rocked in the fury of the election campaign, the endless torchlight parades and political oratory.

There was one thing that gave the Republicans high hopes. At its national convention the Democratic party had split. The Northern Democrats nominated Stephen A. Douglas and the Southern Democrats John C. Breckinridge.

Along the Western frontier in the mushroom towns the name Rail-Splitter had a special appeal, and in the East there were many rich men for whom it held personal memories. The name held all the texture of a hand-wrought world of wood and homespun, of gray barns and weathered snake fences, of hand-split shingles and old yellowed Bibles.

Out of the Wilderness — November 6, 1860

THE oilcloth capes of the Wide-Awakes, as the Lincoln societies called themselves, gleamed in torchlight of unending processions and political parades, chanting to a tireless rhythm:

> Old Abe Lincoln came out of the wilderness,
> Out of the wilderness,
> Out of the wilderness.
> Old Abe Lincoln came out of the wilderness,
> Down in Illinoy.

When the great day came, Springfield and the nation went to the ballot boxes. Bewhiskered gentlemen in silk hats and flowing frock coats deftly checked off the candidates of their choice. Weather-beaten farmers wetted pencils in their tobacco-stained mouths and cautiously marked X in the black circle of the straight-ticket voter, and solemnly dropped their folded ballots into the sacred box, the Ark of the Covenant of Democracy. The rest was a clamor of brass bands, a free circulation of cigars and palaver, the making of fantastic election wagers.

Old Abe sat patiently in his room at the State House in one of his detached moods while exuberant crowds churned around him.

Through the evening he waited in the telegraph office listening to the returns that kept clicking for Link, Link, Link, Lincoln. Outside jubilant processions were roaring the song "Ain't We Glad We Joined the Republicans!" The wildest yell of all came when the telegraph tickers told the news that New York City had gone Republican. At last the news he was waiting for came through. His own precinct had voted for him. Again he carried the news to Eighth Street, the news Mary had worked and waited for through so many years:

"Mary, we're elected."

The President-Elect — 1861

"TELL them if one South Carolina finger be raised in defiance of this Government, I shall come down there, and once I am there, I will hang the first man I can lay hands on, to the first tree I can reach."

Such was the warning Old Hickory had sent to secession agitators in his day. In 1861 a shaken President, anxious only to hand on his troubles to his successor, had read an annual message to the Congress stating that no state had the right to secede from the Union. But he had made no Jacksonian threats of action. Two weeks later the State of South Carolina seceded from the Union. The United States Government in Washington did nothing.

In answer to anxious questions, the harassed President-elect in Springfield stated his three principles:

"No extension of slavery"
"No secession from the Union"
"No compromise of principle"

To the house on Eighth Street came mobs of office-seekers and political scavengers, small selfish grabbers looking for rewards in office as loot and booty after victory. Locked in an empty room over a store, Lincoln had written the inaugural address. A flood of lies, rumors, and abuse was now pouring upon him from hostile news-papers, and his mail contained threats against his life. Within the Government there was treachery in high places. Munitions of war from Northern arsenals were mysteriously moved south. The feeble Buchanan did nothing, waiting only to be turned out. Mississippi, Florida, Alabama, Georgia, Louisiana, Texas, seceded almost in a block. The great Union of the Founding Fathers was being rent asunder. What a crown of thorns waited for a President-elect to wear!

Late one night he sat brooding by a dying fire, talking with an old friend of how the terrible threat of civil war might be avoided. He said he had read on his knees the story of Jesus praying in the Garden of Gethsemane, and that he was in Gethsemane now and his cup of bitterness was full and overflowing.

As the time for leaving Springfield drew near, he closed up his affairs. Mary Todd auctioned off the furniture and rented the Eighth Street home. Lincoln dropped his despondent mood and was cheered at the prospect of change and action. He made a last pilgrimage of affection across the prairie to say good-by to the old pioneer step-mother, Sarah Bush Lincoln, who had loved him as her own when he had been a motherless boy, miserable and terribly alone.

He bent down to kiss for the last time the withered face of the old pioneer woman. With a sense of dim foreboding she saw through the mist of her tears the mystic halo of martyrdom about his dark face. Although there was no tie of blood between this pioneer mother and prairie son, yet a native bond born of the same regenerat-ing earth, the fruitful prairie dust, the living faith of things not seen, drew him back at the final hour of his going to the obscure cabin door for a last farewell. The wind and sun of slow and patient years had fashioned each into a certain beauty of the spirit that was sad and sweet and strong beyond the shape of clay.

Springfield Farewell — 1861

THE family had moved to the hotel, and Lincoln had labeled all the luggage "A. Lincoln, White House, Washington."

On the afternoon of the last day he dropped in on Billy Herndon at the old law office. He stretched out on the worn sofa for a quiet moment, looking at the curious pattern of past years on the dusty ceiling. Then:

"Billy, how long have we been together?"

"Over sixteen years."

"We've never had a cross word all that time, have we?"

"No, indeed we have not."

The talk drifted to old times, and the fun and comic scenes they had shared together in the old Eighth Circuit days. "I never saw him in a more cheerful mood," wrote Herndon.

It was time to leave. He gathered up his books and papers, took his long last look at the familiar office. As they went out he stopped by the old signboard that hung on rusty hinges at the foot of the stairs. "Let it hang there undisturbed. Give our clients to understand that the election of a President makes no change in the firm of Lincoln and Herndon. If I live, I'm coming back some time, and then we'll go right on practicing law as if nothing had ever happened."

At the railroad station next morning, the stubby black engine puffed with impatience. The baggage and passenger cars waited in the cold rain. At five minutes to eight the tall man came through the crowds of friends and neighbors, shaking hands and bidding a last farewell. Slowly he mounted the back platform of the coach, took off the tall hat. The crowd stood bareheaded in the rain. All the gray sad tones of the dun sky and dripping rain were in his words.

"My Friends: No one, not in my situation, can appreciate my feeling of sadness at this parting. To this place, and the kindness of these people, I owe everything. Here I have lived a quarter of a century, and have passed from a young to an old man. Here my children have been born, and one is buried. I now leave, not knowing when or whether ever I may return, with a task before me greater than that which rested upon Washington. Without the assistance of that Divine Being who ever attended him, I cannot succeed. With that assistance, I cannot fail. Trusting in Him who can go with me, and remain with you, and be everywhere for good, let us confidently hope that all will yet be well. To His care commending you, as I hope in your prayers you will commend me, I bid you an affectionate farewell."

The engine sighed, the iron wheels slowly turned. The familiar image diminished and grew dim as the train slid down the shining wet rails, till only a smudge of smoke hung in the air.

Billy Herndon, alone in the law office, looked back across the years, and wrote:

"This long, bony, sad man floated down the Sangamon river in a
    frail canoe.
In the Spring of 1831
Like a piece of driftwood he lodged at last,
Without a history
Strange, penniless and alone.
In the sight of the capitol of Illinois, in the fatigue of daily toil
He struggled for the necessaries of life.
Thirty years later this same peculiar man left the Sangamon river,
Backed by friends, by power, by the patriotic prayers of millions
    of people,
To be the ruler of the greatest nation in the world."

III

Mr. Lincoln Goes to Washington

1861

Half Slave, Half Free

Did you, too, O friend, suppose democracy was only for elections, for politics, and for a party name? I say democracy is only of use there that it may pass on and come to its flower and fruits in manners, in the highest form of interaction between men, and their beliefs—in religion, literature, colleges, and schools—democracy in all public and private life, and in the army and navy.

—Walt Whitman, *Democratic Vistas*

The Arrival – February 23, 1861

IT WAS just before daylight. The Philadelphia train rolled into the old Washington & Baltimore depot. The engine panted slowly in the dim light. There was the sharp smell of coal smoke. The sleepy passengers stepped down amid a bustle of baggage and porters, and hurried toward the gate. Mr. Elihu B. Washburne peered anxiously from behind a pillar at the last group stumbling by. He was frightfully uneasy. What if something had happened? What if Allan Pinkerton was right and the plots to injure the President-elect had been carried through? Because of these rumors, Mr. Lincoln's friends had been alarmed and insisted that he make the journey from Harrisburg in secret. Mr. Washburne felt weak and shaky.

Then he saw at the far end of the train three men pile out. Yes, that was he. There was no mistaking the familiar figure, that strange silhouette, the flat-footed stride. He was safe and all was well, thank God. Mr. Washburne pressed close against the pillar, and as the three came abreast he sprang out. "You can't fool me like that, Abe," he said. One of the men swung a big fist at Mr. Washburne's jaw, but the tall stranger knocked up his arm, saying "It's only Washburne."

There was laughing, greetings, and a hearty handshake. Lincoln's two companions and guards were the bearlike Ward Hill Lamon, bulging with pistols and bowie knives, and Pinkerton the detective, who had planned the secret journey. It was barely daylight when they drove up to the Willard Hotel. The President-elect had come to Washington.

Inauguration

A HIGH wide flight of steps leads up to the Greek portico which shelters the main entrance to the Capitol. Above it the unfinished dome stood amid scaffolding and derrick. It was a symbol of something else, incomplete, unfinished, yet to be realized.

On each side of the portico were sculptured groups: on one side *Discovery* lifting up a globe, on the other a settler holding back an Indian from tomahawking a woman and child. At a window in each wing a rifleman stood on guard and ready. Concealed beneath the inaugural platform at the base of the steps were fifty armed soldiers. It was a backdrop for historic scenes where the Presidents-elect, since Jefferson, had taken their solemn oath of office.

On the crowded flag-draped platform, the tall black figure of Abraham Lincoln rose above the crowd. He stood awkwardly, looking for a place to put his new high silk hat. Stephen Douglas reached out and took it. "If I can't hold his office, I can hold his hat," he muttered as Lincoln adjusted his glasses and began to read his inaugural address. The raw March wind blew the words across the crowd.

It was a message for which the whole country was tensely waiting.

"Fellow-citizens of the United States: In compliance with a custom as old as the government itself, I appear before you to address you briefly, and to take in your presence the oath prescribed by the Constitution of the United States to be taken by the President 'before he enters on the execution of his office.' "

He promised that the property, peace, and security of no section were to be in any wise endangered by the incoming Administration. The Fugitive Slave Law was provided for in the Constitution, and would be upheld. He spoke of a great and peculiar difficulty.

"A disruption of the Federal Union is now formidably attempted." If the Constitution were maintained, then the Union would endure forever. No state upon its own mere motion could lawfully get out of the Union. "I shall take care that the laws of the Union be faithfully executed in all the States.

"There needs to be no bloodshed nor violence," he said. Beyond the normal duties of the Government there would be "no invasion, no using of force against or among the people anywhere."

If there were persons in one section or another who sought to destroy the Union at all events, would it not be wise to ascertain why they did it? "Is it true, then, that any right, plainly written in the Constitution, has been denied?" Some questions the Constitution does not answer—then the majority decides. If the minority secedes from this decision, they then set a precedence of a continual secession by minorities. "Plainly, the central idea of secession is the essence of anarchy. The rule of a minority, as a permanent arrangement, is wholly inadmissible.

"One section of our country believes slavery is right, and ought to be extended, while the other believes it is wrong, and ought not to be extended. This is the only substantial dispute.

"Physically speaking, we cannot separate. We cannot remove our respective sections from each other, nor build an impassible wall between them. This country, with its institutions, belongs to the people who inhabit it. Whenever they shall grow weary of the existing government, they can exercise their constitutional right of amending it, or their revolutionary right to dismember or overthrow it.

"Why should there not be a patient confidence in the ultimate justice of the people? Is there any better or equal hope in the world? If the Almighty Ruler of Nations, with his eternal truth and justice, be on your side of the North, or on yours of the South, that truth and that justice will surely prevail by the judgment of this great tribunal of the American people.

"My countrymen, one and all, think calmly and well upon this whole subject. Nothing valuable can be lost by taking time. Intelligence, patriotism, Christianity, and a firm reliance on Him who has never yet forsaken this favored land, are still competent to adjust in the best way all our present difficulty.

"In your hands, my dissatisfied fellow countrymen, and not in mine, is the momentous issue of civil war. The government will not assail you. You can have no conflict without yourselves being the aggressors. *You* have no oath registered in heaven to destroy the government, while *I* shall have the most solemn one to 'preserve, protect and defend it.'

"I am loath to close. We are not enemies, but friends. We must not be enemies. Though passion may have strained, it must not break our bonds of affection. The mystic chords of memory, stretching from every battle-field, and patriot grave to every living heart and hearthstone all over this broad land, will yet swell the chorus of the Union, when again touched, as surely they will be, by the better angels of our nature."

Seward had written the last paragraph, but Lincoln had reworded it into a finer rhythm.

The ancient Chief Justice Roger B. Taney, who had sworn in eight Presidents, shakily rose and gave Lincoln the open Bible. Lincoln lifted his huge right hand and repeated after him the simple words of the great oath.

"I do solemnly swear that I will execute the office of President of the United States, and will, to the best of my ability, preserve, protect, and defend the Constitution of the United States."

The cannon boomed out in salute. On the platform there was handshaking and a blur of voices. The crowd before the Capitol applauded mildly, broke up, and drifted away to Pennsylvania Avenue to see the inaugural parade.

The shirt-tail boy, the Mississippi flatboatman, the Illinois hog-caller, rail-splitter, country lawyer, Nancy Hanks's baby who Dennis Hanks had said would never amount to much, after fifty years was the sixteenth President of the United States.

The Capitol, with its unfinished dome, was a national symbol that looked down on the wide straight emptiness called Pennsylvania Avenue. On either side of the mile of avenue were shabby buildings, but the north side was the more respectable.

There were shops, hotels, and many saloons. Through the blue fog of tobacco smoke in the crowded lobbies of famous hotels— the Willard, the National, the Metropolitan—fantastic personages milled about on the checkered marble floors, or elbowed at the noisy bars. Politicians, army officers, contractors, poets, spies, Copperheads, and honest men argued, lounged, made deals, and spat carelessly great squirts of tobacco juice in the general direction of the polished brass spittoons that glinted through the thick atmosphere.

The sleepy Southern town had suddenly become a fantastic wartime capital, to be turned into an armed camp, a hospital city, lost and threatened in the gloom of defeat or hilarious and flaunting in the news of victories. It was a city cold and inhospitable to the Western family that had just come to the White House.

But Washington soon accepts its new Presidents as fellow villagers, regardless of politics, and then as neighbors whose family doings are back-fence gossip. As the quaint and melancholy figure of the President became familiar, walking, riding, sometimes curb-sitting on its streets day or night, the city accepted him as Honest Abe, as Father Abraham, and told a thousand stories of his wit and absent-minded eccentricities.

If he cut an ungainly figure riding with his cavalry escort to and from the Soldiers' Home, he nevertheless was an excellent horseman. People looked keenly into his sad mysterious face as he passed in his carriage beside Mrs. Lincoln on the customary afternoon drive. His daily mail contained threats upon his life. There were many in Washington who hated him bitterly. When his friends were anxious for his safety, he was cool and fearless and grumbled against military escort.

Lincoln was fifty-two when he came to the White House, physically and spiritually strong and vital. The thick mop of black hair was untouched by gray. Schooled in politics and the close-reasoned common sense of the border circuit lawyer and morally fearless, he was to be tried and developed into new strengths by the awful ordeal of circumstance. "Circumstances have made me, I have not made them." Meaning perhaps that he was confident that he could do what was right and best under given conditions no matter how severe.

The Lincolns Move In

"PROBABLY no family that ever lived in the Executive Mansion was so irregular in its methods of living as were the Lincolns," wrote Noah Brooks.

The big south room on the second floor of the White House was Lincoln's office and workshop. Around the long table in the center, the seven men of the Cabinet sat and listened to their strange chief read jokes from Artemus Ward, or tell stories that had a point and meaning they seldom missed. Whatever their personal animosities and selfish ambitions, these men all shared a singleness of devotion to the Union, and each was to learn the slow sure steel-cable strength and power of their chief, who so humbly listened to their opinions and so surely held to his own convictions.

So Secretary of State Seward had learned. Mistaking his man, he had sent the President some "Thoughts for the President's Consideration," proposing just how Mr. Seward would run things. Lincoln's clean-cut reply let the Secretary know once and for all who was President and that advice would be asked for when wanted. They understood each other and became better friends.

There were political Jack Armstrongs waiting to tackle him and reduce him to a mere party tool. He handled these mistaken champions more quietly but just as effectively as he did the New Salem strong man. Persuaders and pressure groups soon found under the gentle wit and banter that there was tough oak and granite. The dictatorial Mr. Stanton, the subtle Mr. Seward, and the blustering generals soon learned that there was a man in the White House.

Three of the Cabinet—William H. Seward, Secretary of State, Simon Cameron, Secretary of War, and Salmon P. Chase of the Treasury—had been his rivals for the presidential nomination. He had appointed Cameron and Caleb Smith, Secretary of the Interior, because politicians had made deals and promises without his knowledge or consent.

Edward Bates, Attorney General, and Montgomery Blair, Postmaster General, were famous lawyers. Bates had made a national reputation as the lawyer for the slave Dred Scott in the famous case that rocked the country. Gideon Welles, the old Yankee who looked like a Bible prophet with his great white beard, and who knew nothing of ships, had been made Secretary of the Navy to represent New England in the Cabinet. He was nicknamed "Noah" and kept a voluminous diary in which he gave personal opinions of his fellow Cabinet members and their doings that added gossip to history.

From the two south windows Lincoln looked past the unfinished Washington Monument, down the placid Potomac toward Alexandria and Mount Vernon. With a spyglass "rested on the end of his toes sublime" he could see the Confederate flag flying over the Marshall House in Alexandria. Up the river he could see the white portico of the home of Robert E. Lee.

Tad and Willie installed ponies and goats in the White House stables, and took over the house and grounds as their particular field for fanciful pranks and general mischief, unrestrained by their doting father. Once when Mary and Tad were away on a trip, he telegraphed her "Tell Tad the goats and father are very well, especially the goats."

"Everything that Tad did was done with a certain rush and rude strength which were peculiar to him. I was once sitting with the President in the library when Tad tore into the room in search of something, and, having found it, he threw himself on his father like a small thunderbolt, gave him one wild, fierce hug, and, without a

word, fled from the room before his father could put out his hand to detain him. 'Let him run,' his father would say; 'there's time enough yet for him to learn his letters and get poky. Bob was just such a little rascal and now he is a very decent boy.'

"Tad was the irrepressible spirit of fun and mischief which, through the whole of his father's term, gave life in the White House its only comic element. This lad, the complete embodiment of animal spirits, may be called one of the historic boys of America." So wrote Noah Brooks.

Mrs. Lincoln, as the mistress of the White House, practiced strange small economies, and ran up enormous bills decorating the rooms with fancy rugs and wallpapers, and her own plump figure with very expensive fineries. It compensated for the enmities which her sharp tongue made, but her friends and intimates dwindled until there was no one left but her Negro dressmaker, Mrs. Elizabeth Keckley, the one remaining confidant.

Living in the house, and practically members of the family, were the two secretaries to the President, John G. Nicolay and John Hay. Hay had been in the Springfield law office. Young John Hay was gay and debonair and twenty-three, with an eye for the girls. He kept a diary and commented airily on the great personages and events among which he moved with easy familiarity. He referred to Lincoln as "the Tycoon." In his diary he told of Lincoln wandering in his night shirt into Hay's office in the small hours, to read to him from Thomas Hood's comic works.

"What a man he is! Occupied all day with matters of vast moment, deeply anxious about the fate of the greatest army in the world, with his own fame & future hanging on the events of the passing hour, he yet has such a wealth of simple bonhommie & good fellowship that he gets out of bed & perambulates the house in his shirt to find us that we may share with him the fun of one of poor Hood's queer little conceits."

Another loyal friend was the young newspaperman Noah Brooks. His affectionate understanding of Lincoln drew them together in many intimate talks.

Young Colonel Elmer Ellsworth had been in the Springfield law office. He was the beloved Sir Galahad among Lincoln's close circle of intimate associates. He considered himself responsible for his great hero's safety and had organized and brought to Washington his acrobatic regiment of irrepressible Zouaves who astonished the city with their exuberant exploits, especially in extinguishing fires.

War – April, 1861

THE flag of the United States floated over the island fort of Sumter in the harbor of secessionist Charleston. There was food for only a few more days. The supply ships from New York were on the way. Major Robert Anderson, in command, refused to surrender while the food held out. It was four o'clock in the morning on April 12 when the Charleston land batteries opened up on the fort. For thirty-six hours the shells burst on the little fort. The flag was shot down and a Sergeant Hart climbed up and nailed it to the mast. The last of the food was gone. The fort was a burning shambles. On Sunday, April 14, the fort surrendered. The defenders sailed back to New York on the relief ship. Major Anderson took the war-torn Union flag with him. The Stars and Bars of the Confederacy floated over Fort Sumter. The North and the South were at war.

Throughout the North men eagerly responded to Lincoln's call for 75,000 volunteers, but there were very few soldiers in Washington to defend it.

Virginia seceded from the Union. The capital's only rail and telegraph connections with the North were through hostile Baltimore.

A regiment of soldiers from Massachusetts forced its way through Baltimore, and arrived in Washington. The men were battered and bruised, and four of their number had been killed by the mob as they fought their way through Baltimore. There being no other place suitable, the regiment was quartered in the Senate wing of the Capitol. In Maryland railroad tracks and bridges were destroyed by Southern sympathizers. Washington was completely isolated.

From the White House the Confederate campfires could be seen across the river. Washington was swarming with alarmists and rumormongers as well as traitors and spies. A self-appointed "Frontier Guard" of ex-Kansas Border fighters, under the intrepid Jim Lane, the Senator from Kansas, stood on duty armed to the teeth, and slept on the carpet in the East Room. They were prepared with pistols and bowie knives to defend the Union to the last. Faithful Lamon with his revolvers slept on the floor outside Lincoln's bedroom. Old General Scott barricaded all the government buildings. News came through that troops from the North were coming by water to Annapolis.

"Why don't they come? Why don't they come?" groaned the President as he paced the floor. The whole thing seemed a fantastic dream, unreal. "I don't believe there is any North! The Seventh Regiment is a myth! Rhode Island is not known in our geography any longer! You are the only Northern realities!" he said to the Massachusetts soldiers.

And then they came rolling in—the Seventh New York, the Rhode Islanders, and more Massachusetts Yankees. They had mended the bridges and the tracks and got through at last from Annapolis.

In a few days there were 10,000 soldiers in Washington. Pennsylvania Avenue was gay with marching men, uniforms, banners, and blaring bands. The sleepy little Southern town was overflowing with soldiers. Troops camped in the parks and the outlying suburbs. Gloom vanished in the excitement of galloping artillery, and the jingle and clash of gallant horsemen and marching soldiers chanting a swinging chorus.

"When men like these leave their horses, their women, and their wine, harden their hands, eat crackers for dinner, wear a shirt for a week and never black their shoes—all for a principle—it is hard to set any bounds to the possibilities of such an army," wrote the enthusiastic Mr. Hay in his diary.

The soldiers decamped from the Capitol. Its halls had a spring housecleaning to prepare for the special session of Congress called by the President for July 4. Patriotic exuberance overflowed until people began to believe that one good battle might win the war.

There was a rebel army only thirty miles away.

On May 24 Colonel Ellsworth's Zouaves occupied Alexandria. The young commander had climbed to the roof of the Marshall House and taken down the Confederate flag. As he came down the stairs he was shot and instantly killed by the proprietor. Lincoln wept at the news and sent a touching letter to the boys' parents. "Our affliction here is scarcely less than your own." Ellsworth, the first officer killed in the war, was mourned throughout the North.

On to Richmond – July 21, 1861

WHEN it was known that General Irvin McDowell was going to attack the Confederates at Manassas, near Bull Run, Washington made it a holiday. Society belles and Congressmen hired carriages and filled them with picnic baskets and trotted over Long Bridge into Virginia in the red dust of the advancing army. All day in Washington news from the front was good. Late in the afternoon Lincoln went out for his usual drive.

When he returned, he found that Seward had left word for him that the battle was lost and McDowell was retreating to Washington. All night Lincoln lay on an office sofa, listening to the reports of the disaster, wild tales of rout, panic, and flight. One among the Congressmen who had sallied forth shouting "On to Richmond!"

actually arrived there. Congressman Alfred Ely was captured by the enemy and taken to Libby Prison in Richmond. The possibilities of an army who left their horses and women and blacked their own boots for a principle were indeed boundless, as Mr. Hay said.

The General – November, 1861

THE army adored McClellan, and called him Little Mac. He had been a brave officer under fire in the Mexican War. He was a West Pointer from Cincinnati, and had already won victories over the Confederates in West Virginia. He was not quite thirty-five years old.

He was now, by Lincoln's appointment, General George Brinton McClellan, Commander of the Army of the Potomac. He was looked on by Washington as a hero come to organize a great army for victory and save the nation.

It was soon to be the largest army in the world. No more three-month enlistments, but all three-year men, and Little Mac was making soldiers of them. Old commanders who stayed at their own field headquarters wondered why the General took a fine house in Washington instead of making his headquarters with his troops. His brutal disrespect to the old Commander, General Winfield Scott, had practically forced that antique chieftain to resign. McClellan had been appointed in his place—General in Chief. It made people confident to see Little Mac and his glittering staff dashing about Washington. They felt things were being done. Lincoln's call for 400,000 volunteers had met a national response, and the Army of the Potomac soon numbered 200,000 men. Thanks to Little Mac, they were being trained to perfection. But Lincoln overlooked the cool insolence of the Young Napoleon, hoping for promised victories.

In the West another general was stirring up trouble for Lincoln. General John C. Frémont had issued a proclamation on his own authority, emancipating the slaves of rebels in Missouri. In order to appease the loyal Border States, Lincoln revoked Frémont's proclamation at once, and was finally forced by the General's mismanagement to relieve him of his command.

There were more difficulties, this time on the high seas. Captain Charles Wilkes, of the Union warship *San Jacinto*, held up the British Royal Mail packet *Trent* just one day out of Havana on her way to Europe, and took off two Confederate Commissioners, James M. Mason and John Slidell, as prisoners. Although this made Captain Wilkes a popular hero, Mr. Lincoln's government was threatened with war by Great Britain if the prisoners were not released. Lincoln patiently waited until the popular excitement had somewhat cooled, and then turned the prisoners over to the British. His wise action had averted a dangerous crisis. This ended the so-called Trent Affair. "One war at a time," said Lincoln.

There was still more unpleasantness closer home. Secretary of War Cameron's political past was being criticized by his enemies. A congressional committee of investigation had looked into War Department contracts. There were sensational disclosures of corruption. Mr. Cameron's resignation was finally accepted. He was appointed Minister to Russia.

The President appointed as the new Secretary of War, in January, 1862, Edwin McMasters Stanton. He was a dynamo of energy and efficiency. Personally mean and irascible, he had criticized Lincoln severely and referred to him habitually as "the original gorilla." But he promptly cleaned up the War Department. When Lincoln had to say No to an applicant, he often referred him to "Mars" Stanton. Stanton was Lincoln's No man.

Lincoln's Cabinet, and the politicians who had thought the President "safe," had learned that behind the eccentric storyteller was a man of iron who kept his lonely counsel and stood inflexible on Principle. He was being tested by the fires of circumstance.

Holding McClellan's Horse

MONTHS had passed and Little Mac's great army had not budged. Lincoln and others were urging the General to move forward, to attack, to win a battle. Lincoln said that McClellan reminded him of Babb McNabb's rooster who was great on dress parade but no damn good when it came to a fight. McClellan had the obsession that the enemy outnumbered him, and he was waiting for more men and horses. He was always completing preparations. And then it was too bad to spoil such a wonderful army by fighting. How marvelous it would be if they could just go on parading and maneuvering and being cheered forever as Little Mac gallantly dashed up and down their perfect ranks on his famous horse Daniel Webster, "Devil Dan," without interference from skulking Presidents and incompetent Cabinets.

As thousands of new recruits poured into Washington from the North and the West, the popular General built them into the great Army of the Potomac. Little Mac dazzled the Cabinet and the Congress, even Lincoln, with his plans, his promises, and his importance.

One evening Lincoln called at the General's house, but he was not at home. Lincoln waited an hour. When the General entered, his doorman told him that the President was there. McClellan hurried upstairs. Lincoln waited another half-hour and then inquired. He was told the General had gone to bed. Patient Lincoln ignored the crass affront, saying, "I will hold McClellan's horse if he will only bring us success."

January 1862 had come and the Union Armies had not moved. Lincoln was realizing that his holding the stirrups of complaining generals would never bring victories or win the war. "He who does something at the head of one regiment, will eclipse him who does nothing at the head of a hundred," he had bitterly reminded a grumbler. He must show the army as he had shown the Cabinet that he

would make his own decisions. On January 27, 1862, the amazed generals received "President's General War Order No. 1." It briefly "Ordered, that the 22nd day of February; 1862, be the day for a general movement of all the land and naval forces of the United States against the insurgent forces."

For hours the blue ranks of soldiers went by in an endless river to the blurred sound of tramping feet. There was a flurry of cheers as the colors passed. Someone started up "John Brown's Body" and the troops and crowd picked up the refrain. Young Mrs. Howe and her doctor husband watching from their carriage joined in. "What a glorious marching song, but the words are not up to it." "Why don't you write a better one?" said the doctor as they returned from the long review. That night as the tramp of armies and the refrain marched on in her dreams, a vision of fiery swords and rushing wings beat out a rhythm in her brain. In the gray light before dawn without waking the infant that slept by her side she found paper and pencil. The words wrote themselves. It was a sacrificial hymn of ecstasy and wrath and flame that raised up thousands for the marching ranks of new armies to break in pieces the gates of brass and cut asunder the bars of iron.

Mine eyes have seen the glory of the coming of the Lord:
He is trampling out the vintage where the grapes of wrath are stored;
He hath loosed the fateful lightning of His terrible swift sword;
 His truth is marching on. . . .

In the beauty of the lilies Christ was born, across the sea,
With a glory in his bosom that transfigures you and me:
As he died to make men holy, let us die to make men free!
 While God is marching on.

"Pass Brady. A. Lincoln"

THE President had scrawled the words on a card and handed it to the famous photographer.

Mathew B. Brady had left his New York studio, left success and fame to come to Washington to ask the President to let him photograph the war. No war had ever been recorded by photography. He explained his plan to make a complete photographic record of the war, urging its use and value as a record for the War Department. But all Lincoln would do was give him the privilege of going wherever he pleased with his photographic paraphernalia.

With the pass Brady could go everywhere among the armies. The photographic field equipment, his assistants, and the rest, were his own expense. He and his assistant, Alexander Gardner, became familiar figures where there was danger. From the First Battle of Bull Run on, he seemed to be everywhere, putting on photographic record for the first time what an army at war really looked like.

During the Battle of Bull Run, some retreating Zouaves found him lost in the woods in his linen duster and funny straw hat. They armed him with a sword, which he buckled on and wore to Washington.

He had a habit of climbing up on parapets when a battle was on, to get an interesting view, till a hail of rebel bullets would knock off his straw hat and the swearing captain would order him down. When he photographed Lincoln, somehow the camera looked into the deep pools of his strange nature. Some of Brady's portraits of Lincoln are grand sad poems that tell of mystery and revelation. When he took the generals, he showed the grime, the dusty baggy clothes, the burden of battles on the unshaven faces. You can see the grim Blue armies of Grant and Sherman still marching in the Brady photographs.

After the war he gave a collection of thousands of plates to pay for photographic supplies. Finally the Government paid him

$25,000 for the rest. The money was soon gone, and he remained impoverished in Washington till he too became a relic, a faded daguerreotype, remembering a half-forgotten war, showing a worn card on which was scrawled "Pass Brady. A. Lincoln."

From the center of the semicircle of lawn in front of the White House, the bronze statue of Jefferson looked across the street to Lafayette Square, where in the pale spring sunshine the magnolia trees opened wax-white blossoms. Their heavy sweetness drifted south. In the fall, scurrying chestnut leaves caught in the tangled mane of General Andrew Jackson's rearing horse in the square or roosted in the green bronze hat which the General doffed to the acclaim of the ghosts of horse-and-alligator men.

Lincoln, walking alone across Lafayette Square, smiled at the bronze General, and took comfort. Old Hickory, too, had been a frontier lawyer and politician. It reminded him of a story which told of President Jackson sitting at the Jefferson birthday dinner at the Indian Queen Hotel. He had been listening grimly to the toasts of ardent Southern gentlemen, toasts that had strong implications favoring secession. When his turn came, he lifted his glass, glared at Calhoun with the old battle glint in his eye, and the party stood to his ringing words—"Our Federal Union! It must be preserved!"

1862

Abraham Lincoln give us a Man

"Political democracy, as it exists and practically works in America, with all its threatening evils, supplies a training-school for making first-class men. It is life's gymnasium, not of good only, but of all. We try often, though we fall back often. A brave delight, fit for freedom's athletes, fills these arenas, and fully satisfies, out of the action in them, irrespective of success. Whatever we do not attain, we at any rate attain the experiences of the fight, the hardening of the strong campaign, and throb with currents of attempt at least. Time is ample. Let the victors come after us."—Walt Whitman.

Mars

LINCOLN had ordered the return of the captured Confederate Commissioners, Mason and Slidell. They were put aboard the British warship at Provincetown. War with England had been averted. After the War Department investigation, Mr. Cameron had resigned and had been appointed Minister to Russia. Mr. Stanton of the bulging eyes, the Cupid's-bow mouth, and the perfumed beard, and the atrociously bad temper was now Secretary of War. Lincoln called him Mars. When someone asked Lincoln if he ever swore, he said, "Oh, I don't have to; I have Stanton in my Cabinet." When told that Stanton had called him a damned fool, "Well, if he said so, I reckon I must be, for he is nearly always right," the President said. Once when Tad was hosing the White House lawn, Stanton and the President came by. Stanton was furiously scolding the President for pardoning a soldier. Impulsive Tad came to his father's defense and turned the hose full on the spluttering Secretary.

But as these two strangely different men worked together with all their strength and will for the Union, they grew in mutual respect and good feeling.

In the West

LINCOLN's War Order No. 1 had set moving the engines of war in the Mississippi Valley. Commodore Andrew H. Foote's gunboats pushing up the Tennessee River blasted Fort Henry, advancing as far as the Alabama border. In the freezing January weather, Grant had marched his army from Fort Henry across to the Cumberland and captured Fort Donelson. "No terms except an unconditional and immediate surrender," the Union General had scrawled in answer to the request for the terms of surrender of Donelson. Ulysses S.

Grant had turned out of his bed in a Negro cabin to scribble the answer on a barrel top.

"Unconditional Surrender" Grant they were calling him in the jubilant Northern cities. He was a plain man with a slouching gait and a scrubby beard on a face that seldom smiled. There were stories about how he liked horses and cigars and whisky, that he never swore and hated show-off, political-minded generals, and dishonest army contractors. He had thrown these gentlemen out of camp with threats of hanging. Armchair generals and others complained about him to Lincoln and told stories of his incompetency and his drinking. But Lincoln had found a general who won victories and Lincoln stood up for him, saying that if he knew the particular brand of whisky Grant drank he would like to recommend it to his other generals. The soldiers in Grant's armies were Western farm boys such as Lincoln had campaigned with in the Black Hawk War. They were the same tough breed as the Clary's Grove boys of New Salem. Lincoln understood these people of the Ohio Valley, these rough-and-ready sons of the pioneers. He was one of them.

The victories kept piling up as Grant drove down the Mississippi, taking Shiloh, Corinth, and Memphis, and marching toward the last great Confederate fortress of Vicksburg. Lincoln listened to the politicians' bitter complaints about Grant and stuck by his man.

Heavy as was the burden of war resting upon him, Lincoln's heart ached with deeper personal anxiety. Tad and Willie were seriously ill. As the nation rejoiced in victories, Lincoln stood by the deathbed of his beloved son Willie. All the intense affection of his lonely nature clung to these two boys. Tad was soon out of danger and quickly recovered, but the passing of Willie shook Lincoln and Mary to the depths.

The Ironclads — March 8-9, 1862

A NEW and terrible kind of armored war vessel had steamed out of the James River and was ramming and sinking the great wooden frigates off Fort Monroe, while cannon shot glanced harmlessly off her four-inch iron shell.

Mr. Lincoln had immediately called the Cabinet for action, but the only action possible was to tremble and wait.

Mr. Welles, of the Navy Department, was calm and cool with the confidence of a Connecticut man in Yankee contraptions. In the meantime he was complacently enjoying Mr. Stanton's panic. Welles explained that the *Monitor*, Mr. Ericsson's "floating battery" designed especially for this occasion, was on the way by sea from New York. When he said she had only two guns in her revolving turrets, Mr. Stanton's sour face grew bitter with unutterable scorn. The Confederate ironclad *Virginia*—the captured Northern *Merrimac* renamed—had rammed and sunk the *Congress* and the *Cumberland* and driven the *Minnesota* aground. Tomorrow she would finish off the rest of the Union fleet at anchor in Hampton Roads.

The Cabinet waited in despair. All but Mr. Welles, who wrote of Mr. Stanton in his diary: "He could not fail to see and feel my opinion of him and his bluster—that I was calm and unmoved by his rant, spoke deliberately, and was not excited by his violence." It was one of Mr. Welles's big days. He waited calmly to spring his surprise.

At midnight that night the leaking *Monitor* and her half-drowned crew were towed into Hampton Roads and she took her position in front of the helpless *Minnesota*.

Early the next morning, the *Virginia* in her four-inch iron coat with her ten guns steamed out from Norfolk to the first battle of the ironclads. There was something medieval and fantastic about this sea fight in armor that was to change naval warfare for all time.

For over six hours the strange monsters blasted away at each other, almost point-blank. Cannon shot jolted and dented the iron walls of the *Virginia* and the metal casing of the tin-can turret of the *Monitor*, but never penetrated either. The *Monitor*, with her twelve-foot draft, could move more freely and quickly than the slow and ponderous *Virginia*, with her ancient engines and twenty-foot draft. It was a trial trip for both craft. Every shot and every maneuver was a first experiment. A shot from the *Virginia* struck the little iron pilot house on the deck of the *Monitor*, blinding her commander, John Lorimer Worden. As the *Monitor* drew off out of reach of the *Virginia*, that vessel slowly made for the shelter of the Norfolk batteries on the James River. The fight was over. The two ships never risked another encounter. Later the *Virginia* was blown up by the Confederates when they evacuated Norfolk. A few months afterward the *Monitor* sank in an Atlantic storm as she was being towed to Charleston.

The Union fleet was saved. The blockade of the Confederacy went on. Mr. Stanton recovered his composure. Mr. Gideon Welles had his victory, and the grand old Norseman John Ericsson, the father of the *Monitor*, became a national hero.

The Peninsula

In spite of War Order No. 1, McClellan had persuaded Lincoln to postpone the advance. The General needed to complete his vast plans for an advance on Richmond by way of Norfolk and up the James River. Lincoln was opposed to this route, but deferred to the General. It was March before the army moved at last on Manassas. Here they found the Confederates had already left. The Confederate guns that had threatened the lower Potomac were found to be trees mounted to look like cannon. McClellan had been held up for months by "Quaker guns," as they were called. Little Mac returned to Washington.

The Army of the Potomac, 100,000 strong with its mighty baggage, "my army," as McClellan called it, had been transported down the Potomac, but instead of marching on Richmond, it was besieging Yorktown. Lincoln said McClellan was a good engineer with a special talent for a *stationary* engine.

From the high watershed of the Blue Ridge Mountains of Virginia, there are four rivers flowing down in parallel streams to the great Chesapeake Bay. The Rappahannock, the York, the James, and the Rapidan were highways and barriers for the great campaigns of the years of war. They crossed a 100-mile no man's land of swamp and piny wilderness between the two capitals.

Jefferson Davis sat in the White House of the Confederacy in the capital at Richmond. The Army of Northern Virginia was its bulwark, and Joseph Johnston, Robert E. Lee, Thomas Jonathan ("Stonewall") Jackson, Daniel H. Hill, and Richard S. Ewell its champions.

Between the James and York rivers lies the "Peninsula." It was once the kingdom of the Indian chief Powhatan. John Smith and the men of Jamestown had explored its swampy pine lands. Roger Bacon had defied his royal governor and king and put Jamestown to the torch a hundred years before Patrick Henry and Thomas Jefferson had kindled flames of the American Revolution at Williamsburg. Here Cornwallis had surrendered to Washington and Lafayette and the French fleet.

As the April green and the scent of spring came again to the Peninsula, McClellan's army was clearing out the old Revolutionary trenches before Yorktown, where a Confederate army was besieged. These were both American armies, each fighting for its own kind of liberty.

In Washington, Lincoln waited for news from McClellan and the advance on Richmond. Six weeks had passed with the Union army besieging Yorktown while Lee used the precious days to strengthen

the defenses of Richmond. When the Yorktown defenders withdrew, McClellan advanced slowly up the Peninsula to within a few miles of Richmond. Three days' march away at Fredericksburg, another Union army of 40,000 men under McDowell was ready to join him. Richmond was doomed. In the Northern cities people were saying "The war will be over this summer."

Jackson in the Valley

THE great rolling shoulders of the Blue Ridge slant across northern Virginia, and out of their beautiful valleys the Shenandoah River flows down to meet the Potomac, making a valley highway for an army to march on Washington. As the Union army gathered before Richmond, Stonewall Jackson and his "Foot Cavalry" slipped out of the Confederate capital and marched for "the Valley." Jackson was a tall, incomprehensible, eccentric professor who carried three lemons and Napoleon's maxims and the Holy Bible in his knapsack. He trained his soldiers to march hour after hour with a speed that won their nickname of Jackson's Foot Cavalry. Once an hour the whole army halted, every man lay flat on his back for precisely ten minutes, and then the column swung on tirelessly over the rolling blue hills and misty valleys.

At the news of Jackson in the Shenandoah Valley Washington trembled. Lincoln called McDowell's 40,000 men from the Richmond campaign to go after Jackson in the Shenandoah and sent several other generals from the Washington defenses to head off the dreaded Foot Cavalry. But the wily Confederate fox defeated two of the Union forces, fooled the rest, and got back to Richmond in time to aid Lee's attack on McClellan. Jackson's brilliant execution of Lee's strategy became one of the famous campaigns of history.

Between Jefferson Davis and Robert E. Lee there was perfect agreement, or rather, Lee understood the curious mind of the harassed President. When the Confederate chief James Longstreet had been wounded in the fighting on the Peninsula, Davis had appointed Lee commander of the Army of Northern Virginia with perfect confidence. Robert E. Lee had always inspired confidence through his fifty years as a soldier and a plantation aristocrat in the Tidewater tradition of Virginia. For Lee, "duty" had been first and best of all. His father had been one of Washington's favorite officers. He had been offered command of the Union forces by his revered lifetime friend, General Scott, with Lincoln's approval, but had refused. Lee had believed in the Union and that secession was wrong, but when Virginia had seceded he followed his native state with the mystic loyalty of the Virginia blood. Beneath his courtly dignity and Christian piety was the born soldier who could say of the ghastly horror on the battlefield of Fredericksburg "It is well that war is so terrible, else we might grow too fond of it." It seemed that Lee had the dangerous power of knowing how McClellan's mind worked. He had made McClellan believe that he was outnumbered. Lee's daring strategy and Jackson's military genius had divided the enemy's forces and saved Richmond. James E. B. ("Jeb") Stuart, his boy commander of cavalry, had ridden in a plundering cavalcade completely around the Union army. Stuart's cavalrymen were the eyes of the army. "Jeb" Stuart was twenty-four years old, a gay, singing centaur who laughed and danced and fought with a sure and daring grace. In his ostrich-plumed hat, with his bristling red beard, his golden spurs and gay sash, he was the beau sabreur of Southern chivalry, and the lightning bolt of Lee's strength. Wherever he went he took Sweeney, his personal minstrel, whose songs and banjo were famous throughout the army.

Lee now boldly moved from the defense to the attack. For seven terrible days the fighting raged through the pine swamps of the flooded Chickahominy. Lee drove the Union army back to the protection of the gunboats on the James River at Harrison's Landing.

The long train of the Union baggage wagons swaying over the corduroy roads through the morass barely escaped the pursuing Confederates. The Union force made a stand at Malvern Hill, where its artillery opened up on the disorganized Confederate advance and shattered the Confederate charges with such awful slaughter that Lee's army finally drew back to Richmond. It was said that a Union counterattack at this time could easily have taken Richmond.

A change had come over Lincoln as he grew in his slow way. He no longer was holding McClellan's stirrup waiting for a victory. Now he knew that the General had none to give. He had seen something of war and the generals. He had studied military tactics as he had once mastered surveying. From now on he would make his own decisions boldly. The Peninsula campaign was over. McClellan seemed lost in his own complacent blundering. Lincoln said this reminded him of the visitor to the jail who got lost and asked an inmate in a cell "How do I get out of here?"

Lincoln went down the Potomac to Harrison's Landing to see things for himself. It was a surprise visit. When he met Little Mac, the General complacently handed him a letter he had written giving the President long advice on how to conduct the Government. The man's egotism was hopeless.

Two days after Lincoln's return to Washington, the President sent an order to General Henry W. Halleck, commander of the Army of the Mississippi, to come to Washington to assume command of all of the Union land forces. He was to replace McClellan, who remained in command of the Army of the Potomac. "Old Brains," as Halleck was called, soon became an armchair negation, shirking the responsibility of command, lost in a maze of office files.

In response to Lincoln's call, newly recruited troops were arriving in Washington during the second summer of the war. In states where the quota was not filled by volunteers, the men were drafted. A blindfolded man drew the names from a revolving drum. Exemption

could be bought for $300 paid for a substitute. "Thousands who wish not to personally enter the service, are nevertheless anxious to pay and send substitutes, provided they can have assurance that similar unwilling persons, similarly situated, will be compelled to do likewise," as Mr. Lincoln politely explained this strange procedure. Thousands of recruits swung along to a song with a tune of Stephen Foster's "We're Coming, Father Abraham, Three Hundred Thousand More."

A new army was formed, and a general must be chosen who would lead the Army of Virginia, as it was called, to victory. Lincoln appointed Major General John Pope, who had won victories on the Mississippi.

Waiting for a Victory

LINCOLN's earnest plea for the gradual emancipation of the slaves by government purchase was too mild and too slow for people reading of black martyrdom in *Uncle Tom's Cabin*. Delegations of Abolitionist ministers and fervent Friends came to the White House to tell him that he was the instrument of God's will to free the slaves.

"If it be true that the Lord has appointed me to do the work the Friend has indicated, is it not probable that He would have communicated knowledge of the fact to me as well as to her?" he replied impatiently to an urgent Quaker woman. To the clamorous Abolitionists he wearily said, "When the time comes for dealing with slavery, I trust I shall be willing to do my duty though it cost me my life. And, gentlemen, lives will be lost."

Then there was Horace Greeley, the moon-faced editor of the New York *Tribune*. This paper had been bitter against the Government. Lincoln patiently said it reminded him of the husband whose wife had given him a good thrashing—"Let her alone; it don't hurt me, and it does her a power of good." Greeley printed a letter to the President in his paper, headed "The Prayer of Twenty Millions," demanding that Lincoln emancipate the slaves.

In his letter of reply Lincoln wrote: "My paramount object is to save the Union, and is not either to save or to destroy slavery. If I could save the Union without freeing any slave, I would do it; and if I could save it by freeing all the slaves, I would do it; and if I could save it by freeing some and leaving others alone, I would also do that.

"What I do about slavery and the colored race, I do because I believe it helps to save the Union, and what I forbear, I forbear because I do not believe it would help to save the Union."

This letter answered Mr. Greeley and the prayer of twenty millions with a positive statement of Lincoln's stand on the slavery question. It had the Lincoln style and the double rhythm with which his mind expressed ideas. "His ideas moved, as the beasts entered the Ark, in pairs," commented Senator Sumner.

The First Draft

OUTSIDE the Cabinet Room windows the July heat blazed and shimmered. The President had finished reading the first draft of an Emancipation Proclamation. He had not asked for advice, for he had made up his mind and the Cabinet had learned what that meant. He wanted to hear suggestions only. "Nothing was offered that I had not already settled in my own mind, until Secretary Seward spoke.

" 'Now while I approve the measure, I suggest, sir, that you postpone its issue, until you can give it to the country supported by military success instead of issuing it, as would be the case now, upon the greatest disasters of the war.'

"The wisdom of the view of the Secretary of State struck me with very great force. It was an aspect of the case that, in all my thought upon the subject, I had entirely overlooked. The result was that I put the draft of the proclamation aside, waiting for victory."

General David Hunter, Commander of the Department of the South, had issued his own emancipation proclamation, declaring forever free all persons held as slaves in the states of Georgia, Florida, and South Carolina. Lincoln promptly revoked the order, reserving this measure to himself. He besought the slave-holding states to accept the government's offer of gradual compensated emancipation. "The change it contemplates would come gently as the dews of heaven, not rending or wrecking anything. Will you not embrace it? So much good has not been done, by one effort, in all past time, as in the providence of God it is now your high privilege to do. May the vast future not have to lament that you have neglected it."

The vast future would have to lament. The pro-Union Border States would not agree. There was clamor and confusion of striving voices. If slavery is not wrong, nothing is wrong, but let it alone where it is—this had always been his conviction. In the pressure of opposing factions, he at last made up his mind to free the slaves in the seceded states by proclamation as a war measure.

"The Will of God Prevails."

LINCOLN HAD been told God's will and purpose so many times by both sides that he wondered. His lonely thoughts paused before the mystery—war, the will of God, the Right, the Wrong, the eternal struggle.

"The will of God prevails. In great contests each party claims to act in accordance with the will of God. Both *may* be and one *must* be wrong. God cannot be *for* and *against* the same thing at the same time. In the present civil war it is quite possible that God's purpose is something quite different from the purpose of either party; and yet the human instrumentalities, working just as they do, are of the best adaptation to effect his purpose.

"I am almost ready to say that this is probably true: that God wills this contest, and wills that it shall not end yet. By His mere power on the minds of the now contestants, He could have either *saved* or *destroyed* the Union without a human contest. Yet the contest began. And having begun, He could give the final victory to either side any day. Yet the contest proceeds."

He had never joined any church. But he voiced a clear statement of his practical faith "When any church will inscribe over its altar, as its sole qualification for membership, the Saviour's condensed statement of both Law and Gospel, 'Thou shalt love the Lord thy God with all thy heart and with all thy soul and with all thy mind, and thy neighbor as thyself,' that church will I join with all my heart and soul."

A Yankee biographer has said of him that "He practiced with God the same superb, shrewd opportunism by which, as contrasted with the dogmatic idealism of Jefferson Davis, he saved the American Union."[1]

"Back from the trebly crimson field"— August, 1862

IT WAS the end of a sultry August, and Washington was stirred with the news that Pope's army had met Lee at Manassas, that there was a second Battle of Bull Run being fought, and that Pope had won. The Provost Marshal had rounded up all the busses, cabs, and market carts in the city; even the horses on the new streetcars were requisitioned, to send supplies to Pope.

The next day, in the pouring rain that so often followed a battle, came the news that Pope was defeated, that Lee and Jackson and Longstreet had cut the Army of Virginia to pieces. Alexandria and Washington were soon filled with disheartened troops from Pope's army. Army morale was being shattered, something must be done.

[1] Gamaliel Bradford.

Lincoln and Seward went to the McClellan house on H Street, and humbly asked the discredited General to take command and reorganize the troops. It had been whispered that McClellan had refused to send Pope reinforcements, and had brought about his defeat.

Little Mac was again dashing about Washington on his great war horse Daniel Webster. Soon a new spirit fired the army. They were marching behind their beloved General again, out across Maryland to head off Lee, who after his victory at Bull Run had crossed the Potomac and was moving north. Again McClellan was filling his self-styled role of the Savior of his Country.

Antietam

THE two armies blundered into each other on September 17. There were wild charges across the stone bridges of Antietam Creek. There was fierce fighting among the orchards and the cornfields around the peaceful Dunkard Church.

After the three terrible days of the Battle of Antietam, Lee retreated safely across the Potomac while McClellan complacently announced his fruitless victory as "a masterpiece of art."

Lincoln, bitterly disappointed that Lee's army had not been destroyed, went out to visit the Army of the Potomac and the blood-soaked fields of Antietam. Two days later McClellan received orders: "The President directs that you cross the Potomac and give battle to the enemy, or drive him south. Your army must move now, while the roads are good." A month of the bright autumn weather passed, and the army did not move.

While McClellan was away from his army in Philadelphia, Jeb Stuart rode his cavalry around the Union army for the second time that year. Lincoln said to Hay: "After the battle of Antietam I went up to the field to try to get him to move, and came back thinking he would move at once. But when I got home he began to argue why he ought not to move. I peremptorily ordered him to advance. It was nineteen days before he put a man over the river. It was nine days longer before he got his army across and then he stopped again, delaying on little pretexts of wanting this and that. I began to fear he was playing false—that he did not want to hurt the enemy. I saw how he could intercept the enemy on the way to Richmond. I determined to make that the test. If he let them get away, I would remove him. He did so, and I relieved him."

There was a bitter feeling of anger and frustration throughout the country against the incompetence of army leaders whom Lincoln had chosen. A poet in Washington caught the mood in verses with an echoing refrain, "Abraham Lincoln, give us a Man!" Lincoln read it aloud to his gloomy Cabinet.

> "Back from the trebly crimson field
>   Terrible words are thunder tost,
> Full of the wrath that will not yield,
>   Full of revenge for battles lost!
> Hark to their echo, as it crost
>   The Capitol, making faces wan:
> 'End this murderous holocaust;
>   Abraham Lincoln, give us a Man!' "

"The last, best hope of earth"

ALTHOUGH Antietam was not a decisive victory such as he had hoped for, Lincoln decided it was of sufficient military advantage to warrant his issuing the Emancipation Proclamation which he had read to the Cabinet a few months previously.

On September 22, 1862, the President called a Cabinet meeting. After the seven members were seated, the President opened a book and read a few comic pages from Artemus Ward. Mr. Stanton glowered indignantly, and the rest of the Cabinet smiled faintly and indulgently. Lincoln closed the book and his manner changed.

"When the rebel army was at Frederick I determined, as soon as it should be driven out of Maryland, to issue a proclamation of emancipation, such as I thought most likely to be useful. I said nothing to anyone, but I made the promise to myself and—to my Maker. The rebel army is now driven out, and I am going to fulfill that promise.

"I have got you together to hear what I have written down. I do not wish your advice about the main matter; for that I have determined for myself."

A few minor changes were suggested and accepted, and the document was finished. The following Monday it was printed in the papers throughout the country.

It said: "That on the first day of January, in the year of our Lord one thousand eight hundred and sixty-three, all persons held as slaves within any State, or designated part of a State, the people whereof shall then be in rebellion against the United States, shall be then, thenceforward, and forever free."

This meant that the slaveowners in the loyal states could keep their slaves. Only the slaves of the rebellious states were to be liberated. The proclamation was approved in the editorials of newspapers in the North and Abolitionists and preachers sang paeans of praise and the readers of *Uncle Tom's Cabin* rejoiced, but the proclamation would have to be enforced by bayonets and by battles. Businessmen remained pessimistic, and worst of all, recruiting continued to fall off and desertion increased.

"The North responds sufficiently in breath, but breath kills no rebels," wrote Lincoln sadly. He had played his trump card, and nothing had happened. But he was able to stand outside of the present and the immediate hour, and look over the shoulder of History to see what people a hundred years ahead might think. As he wrote the second annual message to Congress, the vision shaped itself in noble phrases.

"Fellow-citizens, we cannot escape history. We of this Congress and this administration will be remembered in spite of ourselves. No personal significance or insignificance can spare one or another of us. The fiery trial through which we pass will light us down, in honor or dishonor, to the latest generation. We say we are for the Union. The world will not forget that we say this. We know how to save the Union. The world knows we do know how to save it. We—even we here—hold the power and bear the responsibility. In giving freedom to the slave, we assure freedom to the free—honorable alike in what we give and what we preserve. We shall nobly save or meanly lose the last, best hope of earth. Other means may succeed; this could not fail. The way is plain, peaceful, generous, just— a way which, if followed, the world will forever applaud, and God must forever bless."

The Sunken Road – December 13, 1862

IN AN army of marvelously bewhiskered generals, General Ambrose E. Burnside's were the most wonderful. He had been appointed by Lincoln to the tragic post of General in Chief of the Army of the Potomac. He was a big, handsome man and a brave soldier, but he did not want to command an army. Three times he refused the appointment. This time it was an order.

In and around the old colonial town of Fredericksburg, where the little brick cottage of Washington's mother stood on a quiet street, camped the Army of Northern Virginia. On Marye's Heights, overlooking the town, were the crack batteries of Lee's army, and regiments of deadly riflemen lay beneath them in the sunken road. Across the Rappahannock River, within shouting distance, stood the Union army under General Burnside. He desperately knew that he was expected to bag a victory. He ordered the advance across the river, and a frontal attack on Marye's Heights. Wave after wave of cheering Irish regiments rushed toward the Confederate lines behind the sunken road while the batteries on the heights tore them to pieces. There were over 12,000 Union casualties on that terrible day, and the shattered army retired across the river, the dazed General moaning over and over, "Oh, to think of those men!"

To a visitor at the White House on the day after Fredericksburg, Lincoln began to read from Artemus Ward. When the shocked caller asked him how he could do this in the face of such fearful news, he threw down the book and said, as the tears streamed down his face, "Arnold, if I could not get momentary respite from the crushing burden I am constantly carrying, my heart would break!" To another objector to a comic story after bad news he said, "Were it not for this occasional vent, I should die."

1863

A New Birth of Freedom

"And, if we think of it, what does civilization itself rest upon—and what object has it, with its religions, arts, schools, but rich, luxuriant, varied personalism? To that, all bends; and it is because toward such result democracy alone, on anything like Nature's scale, breaks up the limitless fallows of humankind, and plants the seed, and gives fair play, that its claims now precede the rest."—Walt Whitman

Let My People Go — January 1, 1863

THE great right hand of Abraham was weary and numb with gripping the soft paws of the stuffed shirts and the high hats. For hours it had wagged thousands of hands of the unclassified and unassorted great American people. It was numb from hours of handshaking at the huge New Year's reception, when any American could fall in line and file by the President and look in the sad, friendly face and step out the White House window where a bridge had been placed to let out the crowds.

For weeks the country had been fiercely arguing whether Lincoln would really sign the Emancipation Proclamation on the appointed day. Secretary Seward brought him the engraved parchment from the State Department as he sat alone after the last handshaker had gone. He had shaped and reshaped every meaningful word of the steel-cut sentences which said:

"That on the first day of January, in the year of our Lord one thousand eight hundred and sixty-three, all persons held as slaves within any State, or designated part of a State, the people whereof shall then be in rebellion against the United States, shall be then, thenceforward, and forever free."

Seward laid it on the desk for the signature. Lincoln held the chewed handle of the old steel pen in his tired hand a moment, to say: "I never, in my life, felt more certain that I was doing right, than I do in signing this paper. But I have been receiving callers and shaking hands since nine o'clock this morning, till my arm is stiff and numb. Now this signature is one that will be closely examined, and if they find my hand trembled they will say, 'he had some compunctions.' But anyway it is going to be done." Then he scratched carefully his full name.

Abraham Lincoln

It was a good signature at that. He looked at it critically and said, "That will do."

Fighting Joe

LINCOLN had chosen a new commander for the sullen Army of the Potomac, bitter over the defeat and slaughter of Fredericksburg. "Fighting Joe" Hooker was a gallant, handsome blade of war, as overconfident as Burnside was self-distrustful. Rumors of his talk and brag about the army's needing a dictator had come to the President. Hooker read his strange letter of appointment and admonition from his Commander in Chief.

"General: I have placed you at the head of the Army of the Potomac. Of course I have done so upon what appear to me to be sufficient reasons, and yet I think it best for you to know that there are some things in regard to which I am not quite satisfied with you. I have heard, in such a way as to believe it, of your recently saying that both the army and the government needed a dictator. Of course it was not for this, but in spite of it, that I have given you the command. Only those generals who gain successes can set up dictators. What I now ask of you is military success, and I will risk the dictatorship."

So Fighting Joe galloped out to the army that grumbled in the January cold across the river from ruined Fredericksburg. The Union sentinels could hear the chaffing of the Secesh pickets and swapped rations for tobacco across the lines. Fighting Joe brought a lift of confidence to his dispirited army. There were maneuvers, parades, reviews, with a flash of banners and a flare of bands.

Across the river Lee's lean army shivered and held revival meetings in the hills, watching and waiting for the enemy to move.

When Hooker had whipped the army into shape, he asked the President to come down and review the troops. The ambulance carrying the presidential party jolted and lurched over the crazy corduroy roads. The cursing of the driver at his six wild mules frequently interrupted the silence. Lincoln leaned over and touched his shoulder.

"Excuse me, my friend, are you an Episcopalian?"

The man, greatly startled, looked around and replied, "No, Mr. President; I am a Methodist."

"Well," said Lincoln, "I thought you must be an Episcopalian, because you swear just like Governor Seward, who is a churchwarden."

The driver swore no more.

As he drove through the desolation of cleared land, Lincoln

pointed out the stumps where the axman had made "a good butt" or where an amateur had hacked wildly. He remembered his craft. In the grand review he made a strange figure on his big cavalry horse amid the glitter and flash of sabers and uniforms and prancing horses. It was the grand show-off of war: the bands, the cheering, the torn battle flags. Hooker made bragging speeches that always ended with "after we have taken Richmond." Lincoln remarked forebodingly to Noah Brooks, "That is the most depressing thing about Hooker. It seems to me that he is over-confident."

Back in Washington in the telegraph office he pulled the telegrams from the President's drawer and scanned the clipped messages with his favorite comment, "Now I have got down to the raisins." He said he was quoting what the little girl said when her dinner came up.

The Darkest Hour — May, 1863

HOOKER had crossed the Rappahannock and in May met Lee's army at Chancellorsville. For three days the news of battle had been in doubt, but at last it came. It was the terrible story repeated, the news that turned Lincoln's face gray as ashes, that brought the sweat of agony to his brow, that sent him out into the night wanting to die.

Lee, Jackson, and Stuart had beaten the Federal army in a three days' battle. Amid the trees and underbrush of the forest wilderness, the rebel army, outnumbered two to one, had outmaneuvered and outfought the Union army in three savage days and nights of march and battle near Chancellorsville. In the hour of Lee's greatest victory, the South had lost one of her best generals. Stonewall Jackson had been fatally wounded by the fire of his own men, in the dusk of a victorious day. "Let us pass over the river and rest in the shade of the trees," he said strangely to the dark ferryman when he came to the last mysterious crossing.

The Crest of the Wave — June, 1863

LEE had crossed the Potomac. The long line of his army marched across Maryland and into Pennsylvania. Northern cities were panic-stricken. In this desperate situation, Mr. Stanton was appalled to receive Hooker's resignation. Panic-stricken also, he went to Lincoln and showed him the telegram. Again the dark mask of the President's face turned gray, but he replied firmly, "Accept his resignation."

General George G. Meade had quarreled a few days before with Hooker. When they pulled him out of bed with Lincoln's appointment as head of the Army of the Potomac, he thought he was being arrested. It was short notice to take command of a beaten army, and in three days to fight the conqueror.

Washington waited anxiously in the July heat for news. Lincoln haunted the telegraph office in the awful suspense.

Lee had beaten the Army of the Potomac four times; Richmond, Manassas, Fredericksburg, and Chancellorsville. He felt he could do it again. The Confederate army crossed the Potomac planning to capture Harrisburg, but the groping armies stumbled into each other at the little brick town of Gettysburg.

At the end of the first day's fighting the Union army took up a secure position on Cemetery Ridge. The Ridge is a long fishhook-shaped range of hills. At the point of its curved hook is Culp's Hill, and at the other end of the long shank are the Big and Little Round Tops. Across a long mile-wide valley, Seminary Ridge parallels it in a sweeping curve. For three miles along the crest of this ridge the lean Army of Northern Virginia stretched out its thin gray line.

On the second day, the Confederates attacked fiercely at both ends of the Union line, at Culp's Hill and Little Round Top. An attack on the center broke through the Union line in a furious charge that was finally beaten back only because there were no reinforcements.

Lee planned a vast frontal attack the third day. He had taken long chances before and won. Two miles of Confederate artillery opened up their smoke and thunder, preparing the way for the grand assault. The moment for the advance had come. General George E. Pickett went to his commander, Longstreet, for the final command. "General, shall I advance?" Old Peter, as his men called James Longstreet, was opposed to the attack and would only bow his head. "I am going to move forward, sir." Pickett saluted and rode off.

Fifteen thousand men moved down the long slope following the battle flags of the Confederacy. From the crest of Cemetery Ridge the Union artillery batteries began to blast away. Down the long sweep of the sunny valley a Gray blurred line swept forward. "Here they come," went down the Blue lines, and the barking order "Hold your fire, men!" was heard from the officers.

As the surging Gray waves came up the long slope giving the high, shrill rebel yell, the Union cannon fire tore wide lanes of death in the close ranks. Pickett's men were almost at the crest when the crash of the Union musketry from behind the stone wall wiped out the whole scene in flame and smoke. An officer in gray leaped on a cannon caisson, waved his hat on his sword, and died. For a few moments, the blue Virginia flags surged over the parapet, wavered, and then they swept back down the slope. The broken troops fell back across the valley to the cover of their batteries, now almost without ammunition. It was suddenly over. As the men passed their General, Lee said: "It was all my fault. Get together and let us do the best we can toward saving that which is left us. We must now return to Virginia."

In the night the long Confederate columns sloshed through the mud, the torn battle flags hanging heavily in the rain. The wagon trains creaked through the night with their groaning burden of wounded. Lee's army safely recrossed the Potomac while Meade hesitated to attack.

While the jubilant bells of victory rang wildly throughout the North, Lincoln gloomily pondered the phrase of Meade's telegram from Gettysburg about "driving the invaders from our soil." Would the generals never understand that the Confederate Army must be crushed and not just driven back, and that all the United States was "our soil"? Meade had let Lee's army retreat safely across the Potomac back to Virginia. Again Lincoln was "immeasurably distressed."

He wrote to Meade: "My dear general, I do not believe you appreciate the magnitude of the misfortune involved in Lee's escape. He was within your easy grasp, and to have closed with him would have ended the war. As it is, the war will be prolonged indefinitely. Your golden opportunity is gone, and I am distressed immeasurably because of it."

On the envelope he wrote: "To General Meade, never sent or signed."

Vicksburg — July 4, 1863

It was the bearded Noah of the Navy Department who brought Lincoln the good news from Vicksburg. The last Confederate fortress on the lower Mississippi, with its garrison of 37,000 troops, had surrendered to Grant on the Fourth of July.

For months the besieged city on the bluffs above the river had lived on mule meat, rats, and cane shoots. The inhabitants had dug caves in the high clay banks as a refuge from the bombardment of the river gunboats.

Lincoln's faith in Grant had persisted in spite of the grumbling of armchair generals. The people had called for a man and now he knew that man was U. S. Grant.

"I do not remember that you and I ever met personally. I write this now as a grateful acknowledgment of the almost inestimable service you have done the country. When you turned northward, east of the Big Black, I feared it was a mistake. I now wish to make the personal acknowledgment that you were right and I was wrong." It was a good, heart-warming letter for the victor of Vicksburg to read from his Commander in Chief after the months of mud and battles and the abuse in the Northern papers.

"The Father of Waters again goes unvexed to the sea," Lincoln wrote.

The Draft Riots

NEW YORK was the largest and richest city in America. Its population had grown with the rising tide of Irish and German immigrants. Its merchant princes had grown even richer with the war. The wealth of New York and the ideals of Boston made a curious alliance against slavery. Black slavery was morally wrong, and besides it competed with the wage slavery of the North.

But in the swarming tenements of the infested slums of New York City the war was not popular. The $300 draft exemption was hated among the numerous poor, and the draft itself was bitterly resented by the hordes of foreign-born in the teeming city. There were many secret societies organized to make effective the sullen hate that fermented beneath the surface. As the list of names drawn from the draft drums lengthened, mobs marched through the streets toward the draft depots and arsenals with banners saying "The Poor Man's Blood for the Rich Man's Money." The marchers visited the draft offices, wrecking and burning. The tide of violence rose through three terrible July days. Houses were burned and looted, Negroes beaten to death and hanged. The police were routed by the mobs as the orgy of murder, robbery, and drunkenness rolled on unchecked. On the third day it was rumored that the soldiers were coming, and troops fired on the mob. The rioting died down and the mobs melted away as suddenly as they had appeared. The draft riots were over.

Malice and slander against the President made gossip and political capital in social circles and the many anti-Union factions. The curious vindictiveness which democracy sometimes nurses for its chosen Executives was poured out on the head of Lincoln.

The Senate Committee on the Conduct of the War was opening its secret meeting to investigate reports of treason in the White House based on stories about Mrs. Lincoln's being in contact with enemy agents. Suddenly there stepped through the door of the committee room the towering figure of the President. He stood silently at the foot of the table, his hat in his hand, looking steadily at the astounded committee. Slowly he spoke:

"I, Abraham Lincoln, President of the United States, appear of my own volition before this Committee of the Senate to say that I, of my own knowledge, know that it is untrue that any of my family hold treasonable communication with the enemy."

He turned and was gone. The stunned Senators adjourned for the day without comment. The investigation was dropped.

But among the inarticulate mechanics and sunburned Western farmers there was faith and trust in Old Abe. They believed he would do the people's will, and that Father Abraham could be trusted to hold the ship on an even keel. Stories had come back from Washington of mothers who asked pardon for a deserting soldier son and came away blessing Abraham Lincoln. His name was signed to innumerable notes and telegrams that read:

"Job Smith is not to be shot until further orders from me."

"If you haven't shot Barney D— yet—don't."

"I don't believe *shooting* will do him any good."

"Delay the execution of Willie, the widow's son, until further notice. I guess we'll have to let him off this time."

"Release this man on order No. —."

He had told a general who complained that he was ruining army discipline: "Mr. General, there are already too many weeping widows in the United States. For God's sake, don't ask me to add to the number, for I won't do it."

Of a forlorn petitioner he said, "If he hasn't a friend I'll be his friend."

There was Lincoln laughter in another telegram: "The lady bearer has two sons who want to work. Set them at it if possible. Wanting to work is so rare a want that it should be encouraged. A. Lincoln."

In spite of the shrieking editors there were masses of people who believed that an honest, compassionate, and fearless man was their President. There was a look of the eye, a tone of the voice, that said all these things when they spoke of him as Old Abe, Honest Abe, Father Abraham.

He wrote a letter to the sorrowing mothers of America. It was a letter of consolation and condolence to a Mrs. Bixby. He had heard that she had lost five sons in battle. It was a letter for the Pietà of the battles of all wars.

Executive Mansion, November 21, 1864.

DEAR MADAM: I have been shown in the files of the War Department a statement of the Adjutant General of Massachusetts that you are the mother of five sons who have died gloriously on the field of battle. I feel how weak and fruitless must be any words of mine which should attempt to beguile you from the grief of a loss so overwhelming. But I cannot refrain from tendering to you the consolation that may be found in the thanks of the Republic they died to save. I pray that our heavenly Father may assuage the anguish of your bereavement, and leave you only the cherished memory of the loved and lost, and the solemn pride that must be yours to have laid so costly a sacrifice upon the altar of freedom.

Yours very sincerely and respectfully,

ABRAHAM LINCOLN

The Actual Soldier

LINCOLN returned the salute of the generals, but he took off his hat when the soldiers went by.

"Such was the war. It was no quadrille in a ball-room. Its interior history will not only never be written—its practicality, minutiae of deeds and passions, will never even be suggested," wrote Walt Whitman, watching the grim processionals of war passing through the streets of Washington, talking to weary soldiers from the awful battlefields, nursing and comforting the dying in the vast hospitals. For Whitman, the great figure, character, hero, and actor of the war was the private soldier.

"The actual soldier of 1862-65, North and South, with all his ways, his incredible dauntlessness, habits, practices, tastes, language, his fierce friendship, his appetite, rankness, his superb strength and animality, lawless gait, and a hundred unnamed lights and shades of camp, I say, will never be written—perhaps must not and should not be." And yet in the vivid word pictures of *Specimen Days* Whitman had drawn sad and terrible sketches of the flame and darkness and anguish of war, pictures that are sharp and bitter as Goya etchings, and as tender and soul-searching as the Psalms of David.

On his walks Walt would often pass Lincoln driving or riding with cavalry escort to and from the Soldiers' Home, and note the sad look on his face. "He bow'd and smiled, but far beneath his smile I noted well the expression I have alluded to. None of the artists or pictures has caught the deep, though subtle and indirect expression of this man's face. There is something else there. One of the great portrait painters of two or three centuries ago is needed."

The poet who wrote the great testament of *Democratic Vistas* and the man who spoke the Gettysburg Address, the Poet and the President, passed and saluted on the streets of Washington.

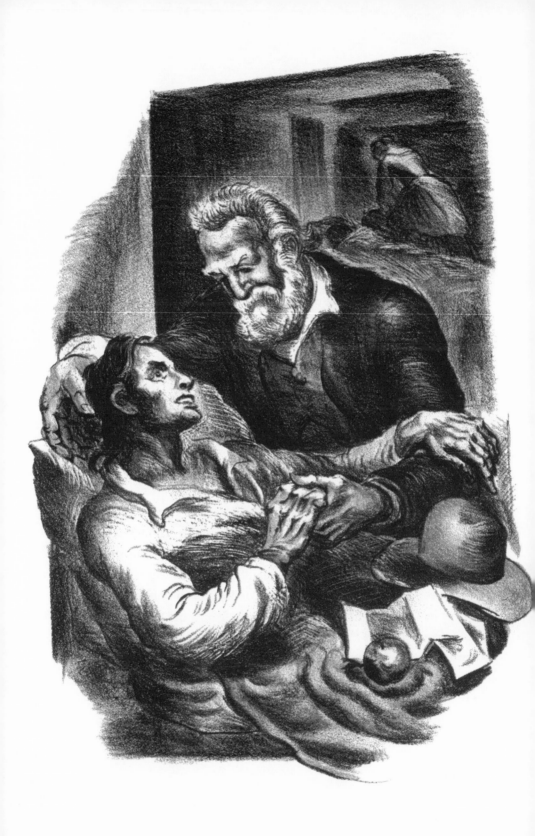

Not Entirely a Failure — November 19, 1863

WASHINGTON sweltered through the August heat, listening for news from Charleston. An expedition had sailed to reduce the "Hellhole of Secession," but under storm of shot and shell Charleston had successfully held out. Late in September came news from Tennessee of disaster to the Union army at Chickamauga.

November came. The bones of the Confederate sharpshooters lay bleaching among the lichened rocks of Little Round Top. The buzzards had picked the bones of the dead horses clean, and the dead were temporarily buried in shallow graves. The battlefield of Gettysburg was to be dedicated as a national cemetery, with formal ceremony, on November 19.

Just two weeks before the ceremony, the President was asked to attend, and to contribute a few words. On the appointed day, he sat on the platform listening to the doleful bands as the crowd wandered among the graves. Then came the principal speech, prepared by the scholarly and distinguished Bostonian Mr. Edward Everett. It was a set piece, long and dull with learning. It was heavy with history, and the sound and fury of Greece and Rome. Only a man with little to say could speak for two hours unashamed before the living and the dead.

When the President was introduced, he arose, put on his glasses, fumbled with a paper, spoke for three minutes, and sat down. The waiting photographer didn't even have time to get his cumbersome machine into operation.

Old Abe had sifted a handful of words to the November wind. They were as plain and gray and beautiful as the weathered siding of old barns or rail fences. The speech was a harmony in gray and brown, with deep tones of quiet earth and the dun sky, reconsecrating human life to the imperishable things of Spirit and of Truth.

"Four score and seven years ago,

    our fathers brought forth on this continent

    a new nation, conceived in liberty

    and dedicated to the proposition that all men are created equal.

Now we are engaged in a great civil war,

    testing whether that nation—or any nation, so conceived

    and so dedicated—can long endure.

We are met on a great battlefield of that war.

We have come to dedicate a portion of it as a final resting place

    for those who here gave their lives that that nation might live.

It is altogether fitting and proper that we should do this.

But, in a larger sense, we can not dedicate, we can not consecrate,

    we can not hallow, this ground.

The brave men, living and dead, who struggled here,

    have consecrated it, far above our poor power to add or detract.

The world will little note, nor long remember, what we say here;

    but it can never forget what they did here.

It is for us the living, rather, to be dedicated here

    to the unfinished work which they who fought here

    have thus far so nobly advanced.

It is rather for us to be here dedicated

    to the great task remaining before us;

    that from these honored dead we take increased devotion

    to that cause for which they gave the last full measure of devotion;

    that we here highly resolve

    that these dead shall not have died in vain;

    that this nation, under God, shall have a new birth of freedom,

    and that government of the people, by the people, for the people,

    shall not perish from the earth."

The crowd applauded faintly and was unimpressed. Lincoln felt the speech was a failure. After the ceremonies there was the usual tiresome reception. But the President found a man he had wanted to meet. It was old John Burns, the little Gettysburg farmer who had put on his long-tailed coat with the brass buttons, and with his squirrel rifle and a pocketful of lead slugs had sailed into the hottest part of the fight to take three lead bullets in his body before he would quit. He said afterward that he did it just to get even with the rebels for milking and driving off his cows.

The following day a note came to Lincoln from Mr. Edward Everett. "I should be glad if I could flatter myself that I came as near to the central idea of the occasion in two hours as you did in two minutes."

Lincoln, comforted for his "failure," replied: "Your kind note of today is received. In our respective parts yesterday, you could not have been excused to make a short address, nor I a long one. I am pleased that, in your judgment, the little I did say was not entirely a failure."

A week later, Lincoln, in his dressing gown and slippers, was under the doctor's care. When the malady was pronounced a mild form of smallpox, there was for once an exodus of office-seekers from the White House halls. There were no more line-ups waiting in the corridors. Lincoln remarked about his ailment, "There is one good thing about it. Now I have something I can give everybody."

Tennessee

THERE were fighting men who sneered at the armchair strategists and politician generals who were parlor favorites in Washington—unshaven generals in shabby, dusty uniforms that smelt of saddle leather and horse sweat. There were Grant and William Tecumseh Sherman fighting to clear the Mississippi and to cut the east-west railroad that was the Confederate life line of supply from the Mississippi River to Richmond. They led armies of tough fighters of the Middle West, bearded soldiers in lousy blue uniforms who sang and drank whisky and dreamed of the girls, or others who read in their Bibles by the campfires and sang the old hymns of faith. There were regiments of tobacco-chewing boy troops who fought through the swamps and pine forests and charged with a wild yell up the cloud-hidden shoulders of the Tennessee mountains in a storm of fire and lead.

At Chattanooga on the Tennessee River, four war dogs of the North, Grant, Sherman, George H. Thomas, and Hooker, marched their men in a series of brilliant charges up the sides of Lookout Mountain and Missionary Ridge in the "Battle above the Clouds."

The day after this victory, November 25, had been declared by the President a day of national prayer and thanksgiving throughout the Republic, which became our annual national Thanksgiving Day. It was followed on December 8 by Lincoln's Proclamation of Amnesty and Reconstruction. This was an invitation and a pardon to all the Confederates who would take the oath of allegiance to the Union. He called it a rallying point for the great work of Reconstruction to come. His thoughts were planning ahead for a healing peace.

The war was not won but the tide had turned. The wealth of the North during the war had increased as the resources of the South had been consumed. Machinery and manufacturing were producing vast stores of munitions and supplies in the North. But the bright flame of valor still burned high in the ragged, dauntless army marching behind Lee barefoot through the red dust of the Old Dominion to the high quick tune of "Dixie," charging through the pine swamps of the Wilderness with a wild rebel yell, waylaying a Union wagon train, starving on a handful of parched corn in the trenches of Petersburg.

The President and the Painter

Mr. Francis B. Carpenter, the portrait-painter, was barging down Broadway with his usual swinging stride. But this morning, on his way to the studio, his head was forward, and his chin sunk deep in his high collar.

He was lost in the grandeur of his idea, his dream to paint a canvas of the great moment, the crowning event of the age—the deed that at last gave meaning to the terrible war, the awful carnage of three dreadful years. In his mind he had grouped and arranged the figures of the drama, the President with the great proclamation in his hand, the seven men of the Cabinet around the table. It was to be an accurate record, just as it happened, of President Lincoln reading the Emancipation Proclamation to his Cabinet. He had almost shouted for joy when the news came from his friends in Washington that the President was favorable to their suggestion of his project.

But now it seemed impossible that it would ever be started. It would take months to paint the picture, maybe years, and he was without funds. Nor did he know anyone who would help. He paused before the door that led up to his studio and stared gloomily at the back of a man who was looking at the prints in the shop window. Where had he seen the man before? At last he remembered. It was the lawyer he had known five years ago in Brooklyn. They had shared their lean meals and high ideals as young beginners on the high road to fortune. Now they were grasping each other's hands in a happy glow of pleasant remembrance. His lawyer friend would come up to his studio. He had been fortunate in business, in fact he was rich, but he had kept his taste and interest in art.

As they climbed the stairs, Mr. Carpenter seemed to hear a voice saying "This man has been sent to you." The painter's gloom was disappearing before a new hope.

Neither had lost his ardor for liberty, for the Union, and for Abolition, and they were glad to find the intervening years had not changed their views. As the artist told glowingly of his scheme of the great picture, his efforts, and the difficulties, his old friend caught the fire of his enthusiasm.

"You shall paint the picture," he said when they parted. "Take plenty of time—make it the great work of your life—and draw upon me for whatever funds you will need to the end."

"Well, Mr. Carpenter, we will turn you loose in here, and try to give you a good chance to work out your idea." The painter could hardly believe it all was real as he listened and watched Abraham Lincoln show him where and how the actors sat in the very room where the proclamation had been signed. Had it ever happened to an artist before that real characters themselves would pose for the picture of a great historical event in the actual setting?

"Never shall I forget the electric thrill that went through my whole being at this instant. I seemed to see lines radiating from every part of the globe, converging to a focus at the point where that plain, awkward-looking man stood, and to hear in spirit a million prayers, 'as the sound of many waters,' ascending in his behalf. It was the voice of those who had been bondmen and bondwomen, and the grand diapason swept up from the coming ages." So wrote the painter after his first meeting with the President.

Day and night for months the happy painter worked on the great canvas that stood in the state dining room of the White House. Sometimes he would sit alone with the busy President, sketching him as he worked at his desk.

"Sometimes a stranger, approaching the President with a low tone, would turn an inquiring eye toward the place where I sat, absorbed frequently in a pencil sketch of some object in the room. This would be met by the hearty tones of Mr. Lincoln—I can hear them yet ringing in my ears—'Oh, you need not mind him; he is but a painter.'

There was a satisfaction to me, differing from that of any other experience, in simply sitting with him. Absorbed in his papers, he would become unconscious of my presence, while I intently studied every line and shade of expression in that furrowed face. In repose, it was the saddest face I ever knew. There were days when I could scarcely look into it without crying. During the first week of the battles of the Wilderness, he scarcely slept at all."

Afterward Mr. Carpenter remembered and wrote down the things he heard and saw daily during *Six Months at the White House*.

When the picture was at last finished, the painter came to say good-by. He found the President sitting on the curb near the War Department gate, writing on the back of a card "Examine this man's case," and handing it to a plain little man who had come to him in his trouble. Passers-by smiled superciliously at the homely group.

"Rising to his feet he handed the man the card, with a word of direction, and then turning to me said, 'Well, Carpenter, I must go in and take one more look at the picture before you leave us.' So saying, he accompanied me to the East Room, and sitting down in front of it, remained for some time in silence." "It is as good as it can be made" was his verdict as the painter tried to tell how grateful he was for all the kindness that had overflowed upon him from the great heart of Lincoln for the past six months. "He listened pensively —almost passively, to me—his eyes fastened upon the picture. As I finished he turned, and in his simple-hearted, earnest way, said: 'Carpenter, I believe I am about as glad over the success of this work as you are.' And with these words in my ear and a cordial good-by grasp of the hand, President and painter separated."

Angel of Mercy

IF GOVERNMENTS ever showed their people pictures of the scenes after battles there would be no more wars. During the early part of the war the Government had made no provision for the care of the wounded. After the battles the wounded lay on the field without food sometimes for two or three days until loaded on jolting flat cars and shipped to Washington.

A timid little woman clerk in the Patent Office had collected food and bandages and by incredible persistence had got to the battle front with her few supplies. She had served hot soup and coffee in empty cans and jars to the bitter army of the maimed lying on the ground in the cold and rain. To desperate surgeons without equipment she had given bandages and stable lanterns to work through the night. The Surgeon General approved and gave her a pass and an army wagon with six mules. She won over the rebellious teamsters to be her devoted helpers. Clara Barton was on the battlefields of Fredericksburg, Antietam, and the Wilderness, feeding, helping, comforting among that dreadful harvest. She was never given official recognition by the Army but she was at home among good fighters. Her father had fought in the Revolution under Mad Anthony Wayne. She had served coffee and read *The Worcester Spy* from the Vice-President's desk in the Senate chamber to the battered Sixth Massachusetts as it lounged in the seats of that august hall. With Lincoln's permission she directed a bureau for finding or identifying missing soldiers and was able after the war to identify and mark 13,000 graves of Union prisoners who had died in the terrible Andersonville prison in Georgia. Her work and her fame grew until today, in the name of Clara Barton's ministering hands, devoted Red Cross workers are aiding the victims of war and disaster throughout the world.

SPRING had come to Washington. Soon the magnolias would send their cloying sweetness across Lafayette Square. With spring came the movement of armies, another campaign on Richmond. A new general was needed to advance across the blood-soaked hundred miles that had brought calamity so often to Union generals. The choice was inevitable.

Lincoln had Congress make Grant Lieutenant General for the campaign on Richmond and summoned him to Washington. Grant seemed the opposite of McClellan in every way. He was a persistent man with a vast patience. He was without brag or glamour. He had the same aversion to retreat that McClellan had to advancing. Grant had come to Washington with his fourteen-year-old son Fred. He hated its political and social palaver and parade. At the White House reception where Grant was to meet Lincoln for the first time, he had walked in almost unnoticed. In the wild inundation of crinolined ladies struggling to see him, to his embarrassment he had been hoisted to a red sofa to receive the accolade of applause. Mrs. Lincoln had planned a great banquet in his honor. Grant had a talk with Lincoln about his plans, and left for the army without waiting for Mrs. Lincoln's party. He had an engagement to keep with General Lee.

In the piny wilderness of Virginia, the Army of Northern Virginia, like a lean gray wolf, licked its wounds and waited, nursing a desperate valor, a fierce courage for a lost cause. It had beaten a half-dozen Yankee generals and was ready to follow with mystic fervor its stainless White Knight, the good Marse Robert, to the last bitter charge, and till the last bullet was spent.

The summer campaign of '64 began as Grant's army advanced into the swampy forest of pine and underbrush that lay below Fredericksburg. The Blue and the Gray armies met near the old battlefields of Bull Run. In the trackless pine forest and underbrush the armies grappled in a wild nightmare of death and confusion amid the bullet-scarred trunks. The fighting rolled on through the burning woods to Spotsylvania as the Gray army withdrew slowly toward Richmond.

They could lick the Yankees in battle, but now they had to fight slow hunger and long fatigue. Without reinforcement, with meager supplies, they must meet unending armies that kept coming on with infinite munitions of war.

They had mowed down the Blue waves as they came on through the steaming swamps of Cold Harbor, a senseless rush of massed troops into the flaming batteries. In the confusion and chaos leaders were shot by their own men, dispatches were lost, the orders miscarried. In the furious hand-to-hand fight through the burning woods, victory hung on chance or accident. After the battle both sides were too exhausted to deal a knockout blow, and so the long campaign dragged on.

Sprawling armies blundered into each other at obscure crossroad villages whose names were blazed across the world in fire and flame as the murderous charges swept back and forth—Manassas, Chancellorsville, Antietam, Gettysburg, Cold Harbor, Brandy Station.

"I purpose to fight it out on this line if it takes all summer," Grant had telegraphed to Stanton. Lee fell back to Cold Harbor, within six miles of Richmond, where McClellan had stood ingloriously in sight of victory two years before.

Again the ghastly frontal assaults of the Blue regiments rushed forward into the deadly batteries and withering rifle fire. The torn regimental colors wavered on the enemy breastworks for a moment and fell. Under the terrible volleys the Union lines wilted, fell back, melted away, and the defenses of Richmond held strong. Between Washington and Richmond, Grant had lost 50,000 men in one month and had failed to take the Confederate capital.

". . . over the whole land, the last three years of the struggle, an unending, universal mourning-wail of women, parents, orphans— the marrow of the tragedy concentrated in those Army Hospitals— (it seem'd sometimes as if the whole interest of the land, North and South, was one vast central hospital, and all the rest of the affair but flanges)—those forming the untold and unwritten history of the war—infinitely greater (like life's) than the few scraps and distortions that are ever told or written," groaned Walt Whitman.

The Crater

As GRANT grimly dug in before Petersburg for the long siege, Lincoln telegraphed in August, "I have seen your despatch expressing your unwillingness to break your hold where you are. Neither am I willing. Hold on with a bulldog grip, and chew and choke as much as possible."

From the Union trenches sappers burrowed a 500-foot tunnel, laying a mine of four tons of powder directly under the Confederate fortifications. The terrific detonation heaved up mountains of earth, and the Blue troops charged into the smoking "Crater." The Confederate cannon turned on their orchestras. The Crater became a ghastly swarming pit of agony and death. Heroic Negro troops with desperate courage stormed the breastworks and were repulsed. The iron ring of Confederate defenses held firm. Grant ordered no more frontal assaults.

On the Parapet

OUT of the Blue Ridge Mountains General Jubal A. Early's raiders swooped down the Potomac, burning and plundering the little Maryland towns north of Washington. The capital was stripped of troops. Every available soldier was with Grant before Richmond.

Within sight of the Capitol, Early's picket lines were firing on Fort Stevens just outside the city. Thousands of government clerks and convalescent soldiers from the hospitals were mustered out and armed to defend the imperiled city. The bullets whined around the President standing on the parapet of Fort Stevens. His tall figure made a conspicuous target. An officer within three feet of him was killed. Anxious officers at last compelled him to get down.

Reinforcements arrived in Washington. Lincoln saw the besiegers skedaddle. Next day Early's booty-laden columns marched toward the Blue Ridge to safety, while Lincoln fumed at their escape.

Deep South

BEHIND the chaos and the wild news of battles, went on the political war, equally fierce and cruel, each war forming and shaping the other. The Radical Republicans blasted at Lincoln for not freeing the slaves, for going too slow, for conservatism. The high sacrament of Democracy, a presidential election, was upon the country in wartime. The Radical Republicans in the Congress openly repudiated Lincoln for his leniency toward the South, and the party politicians gloomily predicted his defeat.

It was for Lincoln the blackest hour of a dark time. The newspapers continued to fling bitter personal abuse. But the people, the unpredictable public, the individual America that plowed and reaped and toiled, slowly made its own decisions. A party was formed called the National Unionists, which called on all parties in the country to support the Union, Lincoln, and the Government. Lincoln was nominated at the convention of the National Union party a few days after the news of Cold Harbor.

Into the gloom of Lincoln's despairing prospects and the awful losses in the fighting around Richmond, came good news from the South. Sherman had taken Atlanta.

General William Tecumseh Sherman was a lean, grizzled, red-headed fighter with a hawk's beak and a hawk's eye. Pushing through the Tennessee wilderness with 100,000 men, storming the heights at Kenesaw Mountain, he swooped down on Atlanta.

He left Atlanta in flames and ruin and marched toward the sea, cut off from all communication with the North. The army traveled fifteen miles a day, cutting a path sixty miles wide through the heart of the South. Georgia was the larder of the Confederacy, a land of plenty, and the pillaging army fed off the land. Hordes of ecstatic Negroes followed the army of liberation. The rails of two hundred miles of railroad were heated and bent around tree trunks—"Jeff Davis neckties," they were called.

Riding ahead of the marching columns, bands of "Sherman's bummers" looted the countryside and rifled the proud plantation mansions. They had a sharp nose for hidden silver plate, buried hams, and yams. They cleared the country of the last chicken, pig, and cow, to make a Yankee barbecue. The smoke of burning barns made a pillar of cloud by day, and at night the dull red fires marked the army's path.

South Carolina had been the first and hottest to want the war but all the fighting had been in the border states and the states of the deep South. It was the Deep South that had first wanted the war; now let her have it with all the trimmings. There was a bitter jest that Sherman had said he would bring every Southern woman to the washtub. The insult and the possibility infuriated the Carolina aristocracy, and made coarse laughter around the Union campfires.

"The Hole He Went in At,"— November 15, 1864

SHERMAN and his army had disappeared. No word had come since they had marched southeast from Atlanta. One hundred thousand men had mysteriously vanished into the unknown.

For thirty-two days all communication with the North was cut. They became the lost army. Washington, the North, Europe, wondered and guessed. To the inquirers Lincoln said, "I know the hole he went in at, but I can't tell you what hole he will come out of."

Thirty-two days after leaving Atlanta, Sherman looked out to sea, keeping his rendezvous with the waiting Union ships. In a swift, fierce charge the army took Fort McAllister in fifteen minutes, and marched into Savannah.

Sherman telegraphed a Christmas greeting to the President. It ran: "I beg to present you as a Christmas gift, the city of Savannah, with one hundred and fifty guns and plenty of ammunition, also about twenty-five thousand bales of cotton."

Copperheads

THERE were Peace Democrats who gave Lincoln more trouble than the Confederacy; Copperheads who pictured him as a bloodthirsty tyrant, unwilling to negotiate peace with the Confederacy. Mr. Clement Vallandigham was one of the loudest of these speakers and his denunciations of the Government interfered with recruiting. He became a self-styled martyr for free speech. He annoyed General Burnside, who arrested him and shoved him across the lines to the Confederates. They didn't want him either, and he was forced on to Canada, discredited and ridiculous. The Copperhead menace was subdued.

Horace Greeley, the round-faced editor of the *Tribune*, was looking for a presidential candidate. He asked General William S. Rosecrans if he would accept the Republican nomination, but the loyal General indignantly refused to desert his chief. Busy Mr. Greeley then discovered that two Confederate delegates were in Canada, authorized to negotiate peace. Lincoln shrewdly appointed Greeley himself to meet the bearers of the olive branch. When it proved that the peace negotiators had no authority to represent the Confederacy, the earnest Mr. Greeley appeared somewhat foolish, and Lincoln had saved himself from another serious difficulty. The question Would politicians press Grant to accept the nomination? was in the President's mind. He sent a trusted friend to sound out the slouchy little General confidentially. He simply wasn't interested.

New problems arose. Desertions increased. It became necessary to reinforce the army ranks with fresh troops. On July 18, Lincoln called boldly for 500,000 volunteers. The politicians yelled that this would cost him the election. "What is the Presidency worth to me if I have no country?" he grimly replied. Quotas that could not be filled by volunteers were filled by the draft. The draft brought out an inglorious crop of bounty-jumpers, skedaddlers, bought substitutes, and deserters.

Through the sordid miasma of politics, profiteering, and draft evasion, shone bright, brave deeds. Off Cherbourg, France, the Union frigate *Kearsarge* sank, in just ninety minutes, the dreaded *Alabama*, the last of the Confederate sea raiders. Steaming past the roaring forts at Mobile Bay, in the Gulf of Mexico, Admiral David G. Farragut, lashed to the mast, had shouted to the captain of a hesitating ship, "Damn the torpedoes! Full speed ahead!" It rang like a trumpet blast, calling through the gloom to brave men for action.

For Lincoln the gloom thickened as politicians and powerful editors assured him and each other that his re-election was an impossibility, and the Peace Democrats and the Copperheads urged a negotiated peace. If he was not elected, he would stand by the ship till another commander took over. When he asked the Cabinet to sign their names, sight unseen, to a bit of folded paper, they confidingly subscribed.

After the election Lincoln unfolded the paper, and read to them what he had written.

"Executive Mansion, August 23rd, 1864

"This morning, as for some days past, it seems exceedingly probable that this administration will not be re-elected. Then it will be my duty to so co-operate with the President-elect as to save the Union between the election and the inauguration; as he will have secured his election on such ground that he cannot possibly save it afterward.

"A. LINCOLN"

He would write letters saying candidly, too candidly, just what he thought—and then pigeonhole them in his files. They made interesting reading long afterward. He was peculiarsome. There were smiles at the White House when the Democratic National Convention at Chicago, the Peace Democrats, nominated McClellan on a war platform. The General would not run on a peace platform. "He is intrenching," someone said.

Black Rienzi

GENERAL PHIL SHERIDAN, the dashing young cavalry leader, was carrying fire and sword to "the Valley," in pursuit of the daring raider Early, who had come within one day of taking Washington.

Early's lean hounds of the Shenandoah came over the mountain before dawn. It was not supposed to be done, for the mountain was rated as impassable by the Union generals.

The rebel yell woke the sleeping Blue army at Cedar Creek. Out of the heavy morning mist, it sounded as if an army of demons had broken loose. The half-formed Blue ranks broke before the stabbing rifle flames of the unseen foe. Suddenly a routed army was running north on the Winchester road.

The firing waked General Phil Sheridan from his sleep in Winchester, twenty miles away. He didn't know what was happening, but something was wrong. He was in the saddle, and black Rienzi, the General's great war horse, was striking down the road to Winchester like a black arrow.

The men he met along the road cheered wildly and turned back to follow "Fighting Phil." The hungry Confederates were looting the army supplies and fell back before the counterattack. The General's ride had turned defeat into victory.

Victory! The word went north in the zero hour. Doubting voters made up their minds to stand behind the Government. "We'll trust Old Abe to hold the Union; Old Abe and his stalwarts, Grant, Sherman, and Sheridan." A slogan went through the army: "Soldiers, vote as you shoot—for the Union."

The drum of Rienzi's hoofs on the Winchester road beat out a pattern in a rhymer's brain. All over the country people were reciting:

SHERIDAN'S RIDE

"Up from the south, at break of day,
Bringing to Winchester fresh dismay,
  The affrighted air with a shudder bore
  Like a herald in haste, to the chieftain's door,
  The terrible grumble, and rumble, and roar,
  Telling the battle was on once more,
And Sheridan twenty miles away.

"But there is a road from Winchester town,
A good broad highway leading down;
And there, through the flash of the morning light,
A steed as black as the steeds of night,
Was seen to pass, as with eagle flight,
As if he knew the terrible need;
He stretched away with his utmost speed;
Hills rose and fell; but his heart was gay,
With Sheridan fifteen miles away.

184

"The first that the general saw were the groups
  Of stragglers, and then the retreating troops.
  What was done? what to do? A glance told him both,
  Then striking his spurs, with a terrible oath,
  He dashed down the line, mid a storm of huzzas,
  And the wave of retreat checked its course there, because
  The sight of the master compelled it to pause.
  With foam and with dust, the black charger was gray;
  By the flash of his eye, and the red nostrils' play,
  He seemed to the whole great army to say,
  'I have brought you Sheridan all the way
  From Winchester, down to save the day!' "
                              —Thomas Buchanan Read

"*Father Abraham*"

LINCOLN came and went between the White House and the Soldiers' Home—where the family took refuge from the summer heat—indifferent to the perils of assassination which troubled his anxious friends. That there might be lurking danger in the shadows he knew well. Riding alone toward the Soldiers' Home at dusk he was fired at from ambush and the bullet took off his hat. Whatever dark forebodings he had of his rendezvous with death, he protested against personal bodyguards. When Mrs. Lincoln was anxious for his safety, he carried a thick oak stick shod on each end with iron from the *Monitor* and the *Virginia*.

"I long ago made up my mind that if anybody wants to kill me, he will do it. If I wore a shirt of mail and kept myself surrounded by a bodyguard, it would be all the same."

There were afternoons when he sat at his desk and listened to the voices of the people. Anyone with a card from a member of Congress could wait his turn to see the President. For hours he listened to the wails, wrath, sniveling, or heartbreak of men and women, asking, beseeching, begging, demanding—pardons, positions, commissions, army passes, and whatever. He listened to a thousand sordid and heroic autobiographies of his master, the People. His Yes and No was the final verdict in humble lives and obscure destinies. Through long hours he sat, dispensing patriarchal justice, meted out like that of a Biblical judge dealing out a primitive justice to the personal appeals of his people. No wonder the people called him Father Abraham. From this living contact with humanity, he renewed his wisdom, strength, and faith.

As the war wore on and the hospitals grew to the size of cities, he would walk bareheaded down the long aisles between the cots, stopping to talk and cheer, to listen to a heroic story, or to hold the hand of a dying man. There were numberless stories of heroism.

"She means well, and it is hardly fair to laugh at her gift," he said to a soldier who was laughing at a pamphlet a woman visitor had given him. "I can't help it, Mr. President," the soldier said, "She has given me a tract on *The Sin of Dancing*, and both my legs were shot off."

He had insisted on seeing the amputated stump of a dying soldier's leg. With streaming eyes he had leaned down and kissed the white forehead, saying, "My boy, you must live, you must live." Feebly smiling, the man brought his hand to salute and said, "I intend to, sir." And he did.

The Approval of the People

As THE wind and the rain lashed through the November night, the President sat in the telegraph office of the War Department reading the returns of the presidential election. He reminisced with old friends, and read from a dog-eared yellow copy of Petroleum V. Nasby that he carried in an inside pocket. It seemed almost that he had no personal interest in his own election.

He was watching the awesome spectacle of a free people who had fought through four blood-drenched years that the United States might be the last, best hope of earth. He was listening as though through the storm and the night he heard this same free people deciding with the voice of free ballots their own august destiny, for a thousand years to come. That night he said to serenading citizens:

"I earnestly believe that the consequences of this day's work will be to the lasting advantage, if not the very salvation, of the country. I cannot at this hour say what has been the result of the election. But, whatever it may be, I have no desire to modify this opinion: that all who have labored today in behalf of the Union have wrought for the best interests of the country and the world; not only for the present, but for all future ages.

"I am thankful to God for this approval of the people; but, while deeply grateful for this mark of their confidence in me, if I know my heart, my gratitude is free from any taint of personal triumph. I do not impugn the motives of any one opposed to me. It is no pleasure to me to triumph over any one, but I give thanks to the Almighty for this evidence of the people's resolution to stand by free government and the rights of humanity."

When at last the news of his election by a vast majority came over the wires, he said solemnly to more boisterous serenaders:

"We cannot have free government without elections; and if the rebellion could force us to forego or postpone a national election, it might fairly claim to have already conquered and ruined us. It has demonstrated that a people's government can sustain a national election in the midst of a great civil war. Until now, it has not been known to the world that this was a possibility. It shows, also, how sound and how strong we still are. It shows that, even among candidates of the same party, he who is most devoted to the Union and most opposed to treason can receive most of the people's votes."

1865

A Man for the Ages

"Though not for us the joy of entering at the last the conquered city—not ours the chance ever to see with our own eyes the peerless power and splendid *éclat* of the democratic principle, arriv'd at meridian, filling the world with effulgence and majesty far beyond those of past history's kings, or all dynastic sway—there is yet, to whoever is eligible among us, the prophetic vision, the joy of being toss'd in the brave turmoil of these times . . . with the proud consciousness that amid whatever clouds, seductions, or heart-wearying postponements, we have never deserted, never despaired, never abandoned the faith."—Walt Whitman.

Black Benediction

"On New Year's Day, 1865," wrote a correspondent of the New York *Independent*, "a memorable incident occurred, the like of which has never before been seen at the White House. I had noticed, at sundry times during the summer, the wild fervor and strange enthusiasm which our colored friends always manifest over the name of Abraham Lincoln. His name with them seems to be associated with that of his namesake, the Father of the Faithful. In the great crowds which gather from time to time in front of the White House, none shout so loudly or so wildly, and swing their hats with such abandon while their eyes are beaming with intensest joy, as do these simple-minded and grateful people. I have often laughed heartily at these exhibitions. But the scene yesterday excited far other emotions. As I entered the door of the President's house, I noticed groups of colored people gathered here and there who seemed to be watching earnestly the inpouring throng. For nearly two hours they hung around, until the crowd of white visitors began sensibly to diminish. Then they summoned up courage and began timidly to approach the door. Some of them were richly and gayly dressed; some were in tattered garments, and others in the most fanciful and grotesque costumes. All pressed eagerly forward. When they came into the presence of the President, doubting as to their reception, the feelings of the poor creatures overcame them, and here the scene baffles my powers of description.

"For two long hours Mr. Lincoln had been shaking the hands of the sovereigns and had become excessively weary, and his grasp languid; but here his nerves rallied at the unwonted sight and he welcomed this motley crowd with a heartiness that made them wild with exceeding joy. They laughed and wept, and wept and laughed—exclaiming through their blinding tears: 'God bless you!' 'God bless Abraham Lincoln!' 'God bress Massa Linkum!' Those who witnessed this scene will not soon forget it."

The River Queen

IN THE spring the myriad armies of the silver shad and herring filled the river. From the banks at the Aqueduct Bridge they were dipped out with hand nets.

Up and down the Potomac River from Washington to the Chesapeake plied the river steamers. Passing Alexandria, where Braddock a hundred years before had provisioned a proud army, they steamed down the broad river bend by Washington's tomb under the green hill from which the dilapidated mansion of Mount Vernon looked down the long river sweep.

In the spring of '61 the white steamers had carried McClellan's army to the Peninsula, their decks crowded with boys in new blue uniforms. They had come back like white ghosts in the night to the Seventh Street wharf with their cargoes of pain and death—the wounded and the dead.

Of all the fleet, the *River Queen* was the proudest, not because of her name, but because she carried the President on his river trips. In her cabin on February 3 five men discussed with no avail the question of peace between the states. The Vice-President of the Confederacy, little Alexander Stephens, and two other Confederate Commissioners talked for four hours with Lincoln and Seward. Lincoln had known Stephens in Congress. He had once written of him: "A little, slim, pale-faced, consumptive man has just concluded the very best speech of an hour's length I ever heard. My old withered dry eyes are full of tears yet."

As the long palaver ended, Lincoln said he doubted if he even had the right to negotiate with men in rebellion against the Government. Someone replied that there was a precedent in history, for King Charles the First had done just this. Lincoln answered that all he could recollect about Charles I was that he had lost his head.

As the Commissioners left, Lincoln said kindly to his old friend,

"Well, Stephens, there has been nothing we could do for our country. Is there anything I can do for you personally?"

"Nothing. Unless you can send me my nephew who has been for twenty months a prisoner on Johnson's Island." Lincoln would be happy to do it, and in due course the young Confederate officer was exchanged.

Politicians and speculators were anxious to know what had happened at the meeting with the Confederates. In Lincoln's presence Major Thomas T. Eckert opened a letter that had been handed him by an acquaintance who had urged him to tell what had happened on the *River Queen*. The letter contained a certified check for $100,000. Eckert would not reveal the man's name, but when Eckert handed the letter back to the man, Lincoln recognized a prominent politician.

When the *River Queen* brought her passengers back to Washington, Lincoln called a Cabinet meeting and laid before them a startling plan of reconciliation. If the Confederacy would give up arms before April, the United States Government would pay $400,000,000 to the seceded States in recompense for their slaves! He had worked out all the details on paper, ready to be carried out.

The Cabinet unanimously disapproved. Why give the enemy $400,000,000 when the Union was so near victory and could take the spoils of war? Sadly the President wrote on the papers as he filed them away:

"February 5, 1865. Today these papers, which explain themselves, were drawn up and submitted to the Cabinet and unanimously disapproved by them.   "A. LINCOLN."

"*With Malice toward None*" — March 4, 1865

THE rain was falling on the broad steps of the east front of the Capitol. Above, the noble shape of the great dome rose complete, crowned with the vast figure of Liberty holding her sword and shield.

The steps and the pedestals of the sculptured groups were black with people. Below the platform a sea of faces billowed out across the park. Their high spirits were undampened by standing for hours in the drizzling March rain.

As high noon approached, the retiring President and the President-elect, all in the one tall person of Abraham Lincoln, came out at the great bronze doors and descended to the center of the inaugural platform. The waves of cheering rose in a hoarse roar. It was the living voice of the people acclaiming their chosen Executive.

He had held the ship of the Union steady through the storm and peril. The Union had endured through four years of war, the Government had prevailed, victorious armies many thousand strong were her bulwarks and defense. This man who was speaking from the Capitol's steps was one who had been raised up in a time of trouble and had endured as the shadow of a great rock in a weary land.

Again the roaring cheers of the crowd sounded a vibrant salute. Just then the high noon sun broke through clouds and shot down long rays of glory. People said it was a sign.

"Fellow-countrymen: At this second appearing to take the oath of the presidential office, there is less occasion for an extended address than there was at the first. Then a statement, somewhat in detail, of a course to be pursued, seemed fitting and proper. Now, at the expiration of four years, during which public declarations have been constantly called forth on every point and phase of the great contest which still absorbs the attention and engrosses the energies of the nation, little that is new could be presented. The progress of our arms, upon which all else chiefly depends, is as well known to the public as to myself; and it is, I trust, reasonably satisfactory and encouraging to all. With high hope of the future, no prediction in regard to it is ventured.

"On the occasion corresponding to this four years ago, all thoughts were anxiously directed to an impending civil war. All dreaded it—all sought to avert it. While the inaugural address was being delivered from this place, devoted altogether to saving the Union without war, insurgent agents were in the city seeking to destroy it without war—seeking to dissolve the Union, and divide effects, by negotiation. Both parties deprecated war; but one of them would make war rather than let the nation survive; and the other would accept war rather than let it perish. And the war came.

"One-eighth of the whole population were colored slaves, not distributed generally over the Union, but localized in the Southern part of it. These slaves constituted a peculiar and powerful interest. All knew that this interest was, somehow, the cause of the war. To strengthen, perpetuate, and extend this interest was the object for which the insurgents would rend the Union, even by war; while the government claimed no right to do more than to restrict the territorial enlargement of it.

"Neither party expected for the war the magnitude or the duration which it has already attained. Neither anticipated that the cause of the conflict might cease with, or even before, the conflict itself should cease. Each looked for an easier triumph, and a result less fundamental and astounding. Both read the same Bible, and pray to the same God, and each invokes His aid against the other. It may seem strange that any men should dare to ask a just God's assistance in wringing their bread from the sweat of other men's faces; but let us judge not, that we be not judged. The prayers of both could not be answered—that of neither has been answered fully.

"The Almighty has his own purposes. 'Woe unto the world because of offenses! for it must needs be that offenses come; but woe to that man by whom the offense cometh.' If we shall suppose that

American slavery is one of those offenses which, in the providence of God, must needs come, but which, having continued through his appointed time, he now wills to remove, and that he gives to both North and South this terrible war, as the woe due to those by whom the offense came, shall we discern therein any departure from those divine attributes which the believers in a living God always ascribe to him? Fondly do we hope—fervently do we pray—that this mighty scourge of war may speedily pass away. Yet, if God wills that it continue until all the wealth piled up by the bondman's two hundred and fifty years of unrequited toil shall be sunk, and until every drop of blood drawn with the lash shall be paid by another drawn by the sword, as was said three thousand years ago, so still it must be said, 'The judgments of the Lord are true and righteous altogether.'

"With malice toward none; with charity for all; with firmness in the right, as God gives us to see the right, let us strive on to finish the work we are in; to bind up the nation's wounds; to care for him who shall have borne the battle, and for his widow, and his orphan—to do all which may achieve and cherish a just and lasting peace among ourselves, and with all nations."

Again the long cheering sounded forth, an exultant accolade. On many faces there were tears.

The open Bible was brought forth, and Lincoln placed his right hand on the white page. The Chief Justice, Salmon Chase, pronounced the majestic oath, and Lincoln repeated its solemn phrases.

The rugged head bent over the Book and kissed the open page.

The solemn intensity of the scene broke as the cannon roared. Their shattering salute echoed against the pillared façade.

The ceremony was over, and the crowd broke up in a holiday mood of hope and cheer. The President bowed, smiled, shook hands, and entered the waiting carriage with Tad.

"Did you notice that sunburst? It made my heart jump," said the re-elected sixteenth President of the United States.

At City Point

FOR ten months Grant's army of 130,000 well-armed and well-fed soldiers had besieged Petersburg. Lee's 50,000 half-starved, ragged veterans held out in their bombproof shelters and network trenches. The whole South was worn and ravished to exhaustion. During four years the North had grown more rich and powerful. Both sides knew that the end was near.

Again the *River Queen* went down the Potomac with her precious cargo, this time the President, Mrs. Lincoln, and Tad. Lincoln was going to City Point, and the front, to visit Grant and the soldiers. Sherman had marched his victorious army north from Savannah to Columbia, South Carolina. Grant had ordered Sherman to come to Hampton Roads for a final council of war with the President. They were to stage the final scene of the war.

Lincoln went at once to the front lines before Petersburg. A Confederate attack before dawn had just been repulsed. He looked for the first time on the harvest of war, the dead and wounded still lying on the field of battle.

Grant on his famous pony Little Jeff, and Lincoln on Grant's war horse Cincinnati, rode out to review the army before the grand attack on Richmond. The bands blared, the colors went by, the army of veterans stood at present arms.

Aboard the *River Queen*, in the same cabin where Lincoln had met the Confederate Commissioners just a month before, Grant, Sherman, and Lincoln held council. Lincoln hoped it would not be necessary to fight another battle. He wanted only to get the Southern soldiers back to their farms and the governments of the seceded states "back in the Union, as if they had never been out," avoiding further unnecessary bloodshed. There must be no malice, no vengeance.

Lincoln and the generals discussed the peace terms to be drawn up when the Confederates surrendered. They must be generous—no vindictive punishments, no humiliations. Lincoln was looking far into the future, toward a strong and united people, a new birth of freedom.

Babylon Has Fallen

"I ADVISE that all preparations be made for leaving Richmond tonight," Lee had telegraphed Jefferson Davis as the retreating Gray army abandoned the trenches before Petersburg.

Loaded horses, wagons, buggies, carriages of the evacuating government and citizens, poured out of the doomed city. Through the night the heavy detonations as the bridges were dynamited and the roar and crackle of exploding munition storages made an awful orchestra. Famished looters broke into food storehouses and dipped whisky in pitchers out of the running gutters. The great cotton warehouses were fired, and the flames spread through the lurid night.

"We took Richmond at 8:15 this morning," clicked the telegraph in the Washington War Office. It was the first telegraph message from Richmond in four years. The boom of the eight-hundred-gun salute ordered by the exuberant Secretary Stanton called Washington to wild rejoicing. The day was a bedlam of celebration throughout the nation, an orgy of the American people letting off steam. In Washington there were innumerable parades, speeches, blaring of bands, and flags everywhere. The government departments closed, and it was the people's day. Noah Brooks, describing scenes on the night of celebration, said: "I saw one big, sedate Vermonter, chief of an executive bureau, standing on the corner of F and Fourteenth streets, with owlish gravity giving away fifty-cent 'shin plasters' (fractional currency) to every colored person who came past him, brokenly saying with each gift, 'Babylon has fallen!' "

Jeff Davis's Chair

SMOKE from a peaceful hearth rises clear and blue across the valley. Smoke of a leaf fire is a dusty white drift with a sharp sweet smell, but smoke from a burning city is a twisted black column, a writhing monster, sulphurous yellow and poisonous brown. The red flames still licked the gaping windows and shattered walls of the ruined warehouses. Frightened women and children remained indoors. The streets of Richmond were empty.

The *River Queen* had brought Lincoln to City Point and he had been taken by barge to the Richmond water front. As Lincoln landed, with little Tad and an escort of ten armed sailors, frantic Negroes prostrated themselves before him, kissed his hands, blessing and hailing him as their deliverer. As the party marched through the streets the sidewalks and windows filled with silent people to see the man whom they had hated bitterly through four years of war.

The gaunt figure that towered above the strange group as they marched into the fallen city was an easy target for a hidden enemy, and the city might well be full of such. The procession marched past grim Libby Prison to the deserted Executive Mansion of the Confederacy. Lincoln sat in the chair in which Jefferson Davis had presided as President of the Confederacy. The act was a symbol of the end of a bitter hope and the beginning of a new birth of freedom. It had cost hundreds of thousands of lives for these two men to occupy that chair. In ten days the chair in the White House too would be empty. The burning city, the black hosannahs, the silent watchers, the tall dark pilgrim marching through the silent streets to sit in an abandoned seat, himself so soon to keep a rendezvous with death, made a strange pantomime.

Farewell to Arms

THE lean, ragged Army of Northern Virginia had evacuated Richmond in a running fight. The Iron Wheels and the Golden Hoofs of the Machine Age had overtaken the Romantics. The world of the plantation patriarchs was crumbling with the walls of Richmond. A lost dream was vanishing in the smoke of the burning city.

Without food, supplies, ammunition, lacking everything but valor, Lee's gallant army retreated before hunger. The only rations for horses and men were a few handfuls of parched corn. Would one more desperate battle of five to one, be of any use? The Confederate generals decided it would not. Generals Lee and Grant exchanged notes to meet at Appomattox Court House.

Lee was there first. As Grant and his staff came in, the gallant white-haired figure in the perfect uniform, with only one attendant, stood in the room crowded with blue-clad officers. Lee was fifty-three and Grant forty-two. Behind the mask of small talk about the old days of the Mexican War, each had his thoughts. Then Lee came suddenly to the point, to what he would rather die a thousand deaths than say, and yet it must be said.

"I suppose, General Grant, that the object of our present meeting is fully understood. I asked to see you to ascertain upon what terms you would receive the surrender of my army."

Grant briefly sketched the terms. Lee nodded, asking that Grant write them out.

Rapidly, carefully, Grant penciled the terms on his manifold order book and handed it to Lee. The officers and men were to be paroled and disqualified from taking up arms again until properly exchanged, and all arms, ammunition, and supplies were to be delivered up as captured property. "This will not embrace the side arms of the officers, nor their private horses or baggage. This done, each officer and man will be allowed to return to his home, not to be disturbed by the United States authorities so long as they observe their paroles and the laws in force where they may reside."

Lee's stern countenance changed as he read the generous words.

"This will have a very happy effect upon my army," he said.

When Grant asked for further suggestions, Lee paused. "There is one thing I would like to mention." In his army, he explained, the men owned their own horses. "Will they be permitted to retain their horses?"

Grant replied: "I will not change the terms as now written, but I will instruct the officers I shall appoint to receive the paroles to let all the men who claim to own a horse or mule take the animals home with them to work their little farms."

"This will be very gratifying and will do much toward conciliating our people," said General Lee.

As Lee mounted his loved gray charger Traveller and rode sadly away, Grant and his officers lifted their hats in salute and tribute to the heroic soldier who was now no longer the enemy.

Palm Sunday

"SOME of Shakespeare's plays I have never read; while others I have gone over perhaps as frequently as any unprofessional reader. Among the latter are *Lear, Richard III, Henry VIII, Hamlet*, and especially *Macbeth*. I think nothing equals *Macbeth*. It is wonderful."

As the *River Queen* plowed smoothly up the Potomac, between the April beauty of its hills, Lincoln forgot the armies and the outcome of battles. All day the talk had been about literature, and he had read aloud for hours to friends from a volume of Shakespeare's plays. Macbeth was speaking with a soft Kentucky drawl. He read and reread the lines, and paused to admire and comment here and there on favorite passages.

Lincoln read the majestic lines of the gloomy legend as another play was ending across the Virginia hills where Lee and Grant were sitting in the little room at Appomattox. As the *River Queen* passed the lovely slopes of Mount Vernon Lincoln gazed at the long white portico and the scene that Washington had loved. His thoughts may have gone back across four years to Springfield and the words of his farewell on a cold gray morning.

"I now leave, not knowing when or whether ever I may return, with a task before me greater than that which rested upon Washington." This day the great task was almost done. Through the lean worn mask of his tired features, a transcendent light of the spirit shone victorious. He woke from the reverie saying, "Springfield! How happy, four years hence, will I be to return there in peace and tranquillity!"

The white steamer moored at the Seventh Street wharf, and the President's party drove to the White House. From there he went at once to Seward's home to comfort the stricken Secretary. While Lincoln was at Richmond, Seward had been cruelly hurt in an accident as he was riding in his carriage.

The Captured Tune

IN the rainy dawn of the next morning the guns were booming, shaking and breaking with their vibrations the windows in Lafayette Square. It was the five-hundred-gun salute announcing to Washington the surrender of Lee's army. In the Treasury Department Building the clerks assembled in the corridors and sang "Old Hundred" and then marched to the White House and serenaded the President at breakfast with "The Star-spangled Banner."

All Washington was marching down to the White House lawn to demand a speech. Tad had been asking for flags, and the President sent a note to Stanton: "Tad wants some flags. Can he be accommodated?" Tad had been accommodated, and was waving a captured Confederate banner from a window while the crowd cheered. When the President appeared at the window, the crowd went wild, and the air was filled with hats. He would only say that he would announce a formal speech later. "I will have nothing to say if you dribble it out of me now."

He called on the band to play "Dixie," which he said had been captured from the Confederates, and was now lawful Union property.

The Last Speech

THE next night the White House lawn was a vast sea of faces, flags and hats, thumping bands, waving banners, and cheers. When the President appeared at the familiar window, the crowd burst into a wild yell. "There was something terrible in the enthusiasm with which the beloved Chief Magistrate was received. Cheers upon cheers, wave after wave of applause, rolled up, the President patiently standing quiet until it was all over."

He had written the speech out carefully to read, because he had been criticized when he spoke without preparation for using the plain speech of common talk, such as "the rebels turned tail and ran."

Standing behind the window drapery, Noah Brooks held a candle for him to read by. At his feet Tad scrambled for the sheets as he dropped them one by one.

It was not a victory speech at all. He seemed not to be talking to the whooping crowd below him, but to the future. He was talking about bringing the seceded States back into proper relation with the Union as if they had never been out.

"I believe that it is not only possible, but in fact easier, to do this without deciding or even considering whether these States have ever been out of the Union, than with it. Finding themselves safely at home, it would be utterly immaterial whether they had ever been abroad. Let us join in doing all the acts necessary to restoring the proper practical relations between these States and the Union."

Louisiana had adopted a constitution "giving the benefit of public schools equally to black and white, and empowering the legislature to confer the elective franchise upon the colored man. What has been said of Louisiana will apply generally to other States." That was the principle. The details would be worked out to fit individual cases.

It was a cool sweet wind of peace and promise blowing over the hot embers of unextinguished fires of hate. It was mercy and justice and truth speaking out to intolerance, vengeance, and bitterness.

The crowd applauded and departed to more exuberant celebration. The last rocket trailed into the sky, the lights in the Capitol and the White House were extinguished. The dark night wind in the magnolia blossoms whispered "Three more days."

The Last Day

AT the eleven o'clock Cabinet meeting on April 14, Lincoln welcomed the slouchy little General from Appomattox. It was

Grant's first meeting with the President and the Cabinet together. He was the guest of honor. There was friendly discussion of the great problems of Reconstruction. "I hope there will be no persecution, no bloody work after the war is over. No one need expect me to take any part in hanging or killing those men, even the worst of them," Lincoln said.

News was expected from Sherman of the surrender of Johnston. The President said that he felt there would be good news soon, because last night he dreamed the dream that often came to him before great battles and victories. He had stood alone on the deck of a mysterious ship driving rapidly on to a dark and unknown shore. It was always the same dream that came before some great crisis.

In the afternoon he took a long and happy drive with Mrs. Lincoln. "I never felt so happy in my life," he said as they spoke of days to come after four more years of toil in the White House, things they had always wanted to do—a trip to Europe she had always longed for, and a farm back in Illinois near the Sangamon.

A party at the theater had been arranged, and General and Mrs. Grant invited, but the Grants had declined at the last moment and other arrangements had to be decided on. Though Lincoln loved the theater, the rhythm of Shakespeare or the fun and wit of good clowning, this night he was oddly reluctant and did not wish to go.

Faithful Lamon was away on a trip to Richmond. Before going he had begged a promise from Lincoln not to go out in public at night until Lamon got back. Lincoln went to the telegraph office and asked Stanton to let his friend Major Eckert come with the theater party. "Well, Stanton, I have seen Eckert break five pokers, one after the other, over his arm, and I am thinking he would be the kind of man to go with me this evening. May I take him?"

But Stanton had ordered Eckert to work that night, and he declined Lincoln's gentle urging.

"Very well, I shall take Major Rathbone along, because Stanton insists upon having someone to protect me; but I should much rather have you, Major, since I know you can break a poker over your arm."

In the evening just before leaving for the theater, he wrote a note of appointment with an old friend for the next morning.

April 14, 1865

Allow Mr. Ashmun

& friend to come in

at 9 A.M. tomorrow—

A. Lincoln.

The only guests in the waiting carriage were a young couple, Major Henry R. Rathbone and his fiancée, Miss Clara Harris.

The End of the Play

THE curtains of the President's box at Ford's Theatre made a shadowy frame for the dark silhouette of his head against the soft glow of the lighted stage. He sat leaning back easily in the upholstered rocker, with Mary beside him resting against his arm. Idly he followed the trivial jesting of the mediocre comedy. The antic play made a dream within a dream that was vague and restful.

The dark and light of fifty years made a pattern like a play, a strange drama of sharp and sudden contrasts: the haunting image of his dark-haired mother, the Indiana farms, the yellow river, New Salem memories and the golden-haired Ann, the Springfield law office, Mary and the children, the Eighth Street home, and Herndon sitting across the shabby green table, the obscure years and then the trumpets calling the challenge to Douglas and the seven great battles, the great debates.

Rivers of faces flowing by to a droning song, "Old Abe Lincoln came out of the Wilderness, down in Illinois." For four years in the glare of history he had held the ship on an even keel through dark waters, and now the Union was to be reborn, the old wounds were to be healed and forgotten, the seceded States to be welcomed back as if they had never been out of the Union. He felt suddenly cold, unprotected, and rising, took his coat and drew it around his shoulders.

The shiftless guard at the box door had ambled out to get a drink at a neighboring saloon. Through the unguarded door moved a shadow of death and hate, a poisonous essence of malice, to kill from behind, and in the dark.

A flash, a report, a bullet to the brain.

The killer slashed at Major Rathbone with a long knife, leaped from the box, and fell heavily to the stage as his spur caught in the folds of the flag draped on the box. Above the stunned confusion he shrieked some gibberish that sounded like "*Sic semper tyrannis,*" and stumbled out through the wings to make a desperate ride to meet violent death.

A young army surgeon, Dr. Charles A. Leale, took charge of the unconscious but still living body of Lincoln, and for nine hours held guard and vigil while life remained. Four soldiers in blue uniforms helped to carry the President out of the theater, through the crowd, across the cobblestones of Tenth Street to a little brick house, where Lincoln was placed on a bed in a small first-floor room.

As the terrible news spread throughout the city, Senator Sumner, Stanton, other Cabinet members, doctors, and Robert Lincoln crowded into the little room to stand at the bedside. The young surgeon and the doctors did what little could be done, knowing that the President was beyond human power to help. Dr. Leale held the right hand of the dying man as a sign of comfort. In the darkness he would know a friend was there. He had been a great friend of the friendless. He had said "If he hasn't a friend I'll be his friend."

At seven twenty-two by his watch, Dr. Leale signed to the tear-stained faces around the bed that it was over.

"Now he belongs to the ages," said Stanton, according to the legend. Outside another day was breaking in the gray April rain.

Walt Whitman, singing of grief and of the ever recurring spring, chanted a sad tender hymn for America remembering Abraham Lincoln:

"When lilacs last in the dooryard bloom'd,
And the great star early droop'd in the western sky in the night,
I mourn'd, and yet shall mourn with ever-returning spring.

Ever-returning spring, trinity sure to me you bring,
Lilac blooming perennial and drooping star in the west,
And thought of him I love.

*　　*

In the dooryard fronting an old farm-house near the white-
    wash'd palings,
Stands the lilac-bush tall-growing with heart-shaped leaves of
    rich green,
With many a pointed blossom rising delicate, with the perfume
    strong I love,
With every leaf a miracle—and from this bush in the door-
    yard,
With delicate-color'd blossoms and heart-shaped leaves of rich
    green,
A sprig with its flower I break."

Index